Sumatra with the

Seven Churches

Advancing the Ministries of the Gospel

AMG *Publishers*

God's Word to you is our highest calling.

SANDRA GLAHN

CRICKETT KEETH

Coffee Cup Bible Studies
Sumatra with the Seven Churches

Copyright © 2011 by Sandra L. Glahn
Published by AMG Publishers, Inc.

Published in association with the MacGregor Literary Agency
2373 NW 185th Ave., Suite 165
Hillsboro, OR 97124

ISBN 13: 978-0-89957-237-6
First Printing—March 2011

Cover Design: Bryan Woodlief, Chattanooga, TN
Interior Design: PerfecType, Nashville, TN
Edited by Diane Stortz and Rick Steele

Printed in the United States of America
16 15 14 13 12 11 –CH– 7 6 5 4 3 2 1

ACKNOWLEDGMENTS

From Sandra
Thank you . . .

- Gary, my love—for your unswerving support once again.
- Ken Mauger, Elliot Green, David Lowery, John Grassmick, and Dan Wallace—for laboring to teach me Greek. χαρὶ τῷ θεῷ.
- Members of Biblical Studies Press (bible.org) and translators of the NET Bible—for your help, apart from which the Coffee Cup Bible Studies series would not be possible. Thank you for laboring without compensation so others might grow in the Word. May God reward you in this life and the next.
- Chip MacGregor—for representing me with enthusiasm and with good humor.
- Rick Steele of AMG—for your expertise in both the biblical text and in editing content.
- Kim Till of Dallas Theological Seminary—for tenaciously working out the logistics for me to research on location.
- Randy Howard—for helping to make possible the site visit to Thyatira.
- Thanks also to my prayer team. May the Lord reward in public what you have done in secret.

From Crickett

Thank you . . .

- The women of the Heart to Heart Bible Study at First Evangelical Church in Memphis—for encouraging me to write this study and also for testing it.
- Beverly Dickens and Susan Nelson—for your many hours of proofing and editing.

INTRODUCTION TO THE
COFFEE CUP BIBLE STUDY SERIES

The precepts of the LORD are right, rejoicing the heart;
The commandment of the LORD is pure, enlightening the eyes
(Psalm 19:8 NASB).

Congratulations! You have chosen wisely. By electing to study the Bible, you are choosing to spend time learning that which will rejoice the heart and enlighten the eyes.

And while any study in the Bible is time well spent, the Coffee Cup Bible Studies series has some unique elements. So before we get started, let's consider some of them to help you maximize your study time.

About coffee. You don't have to like coffee to use this series for regular Bible study. Tea works too. So does milk. Or water. Or nothing. But embrace the metaphor: take a "coffee break"—a bit of downtime away from the routine. Let it refresh you. You can imbibe alone, but you might enjoy the process even more with a group. More about that coming up.

Life rhythms. Most participants in Bible studies say they find it easier to keep up on weekdays than on weekends, when the routine changes. So all Coffee Cup Bible Studies contain weekday Bible study questions that require active involvement, but weekend segments consist instead of short readings that kick off and make application of the week's study. Still, the specified days as laid out here serve as mere suggestions. Some people prefer to attend a Bible study one day and follow a four-day-per-week study schedule along with weekend readings. Others prefer to take twice as long to get through the book, cutting each day's selection roughly in half. Adapt the structure of days to fit your own needs.

Community. While the study is designed in such a way that you can complete it individually, it's also designed for group use. Because Bible study in community provides support and insight beyond what you will experience on your own, consider going through this book with a few others. If you don't already belong to a Bible study group, why not invite a few friends and start one?

Aesthetics. At the author's Web site (www.aspire2.com) in a section designed for the Coffee Cup series, you will find links to art relating to each study. For this specific study you'll discover photos of places such as ancient Pergamum and Sardis. You'll also find links to videos, recommended commentaries, art based on the Book of Revelation, and other resource material. The more senses you engage in your interaction with God's truth, the better you will remember it, apply it, and enjoy it.

Convenience. Rather than turning in your Bible to find the passages for study, you'll find the entire text for each day included in this Coffee Cup Bible Studies book. While it's important to know your way around the Bible, the series is designed so you can stash your study book in a purse, diaper bag, briefcase, or backpack and have everything you need. It's easy to use on the subway, in a waiting room, at a coffee shop, or on your lunch break.

Why does the Coffee Cup series use the *NET Bible* translation? Accessible online from anywhere in the world, the *NET* (New English Translation) *Bible* is a contemporary translation from the ancient Greek, Hebrew, and Aramaic texts. A team of biblical-language scholars volunteered their time to prepare it because they shared a vision to make the Bible available worldwide without the high cost of permissions usually required for using copyrighted materials. Any other translation, with the exception of the *King James Version*, would have made the cost of including the text here prohibitive. Only through the generosity of Biblical Studies Press and the NET Bible translators is this convenience possible. You can find more information about the NET Bible at bible.org.

Sensitivity to time-and-culture considerations. Many Bible studies begin by guiding readers to observe and interpret the words written to the original audience (the exegetical step) and then to apply the words directly to a contemporary setting (the homiletical step). Yet they skip the intermediate theological step, where we identify what is timeless. The result is sometimes misapplication. For example, Paul told slaves to obey their masters, and many conclude that means we need to obey our employers. Yet today's bosses don't own their employees, nor do they usually share the same household. Employment is by mutual agreement; slavery is not. So we should probably find the timeless principle of submitting to authority (using the voluntary *submit* rather than the obligatory *obey*) before we apply the text to employment. In the Coffee Cup series, our aim is to be particularly sensitive to the audience to whom the original text was addressed, but also to take the crucial step of separating what was intended for a limited audience from that which is for all audiences for all time.

Sensitivity to genre. Rather than crafting a series in which each study is laid out exactly like all the others, each Coffee Cup study is structured to best explore the genre category examined—whether epistle (letter), poetry, gospel, history, or narrative. The way we study a story (narrative) such as Jonah differs from how we might examine the compact poetry in Song of Songs or an epistle such as Philippians. So while the studies in the Coffee Cup series have similar elements, each study takes the approach to the text that best fits the genre.

The reason *Sumatra with the Seven Churches* explores only a few chapters of Revelation rather than the entire book is because the first few chapters of the Book of Revelation appear in a different genre than the rest of the book. The section we will consider contains messages from Christ to seven first-century churches in Asia Minor ("Asia" in New Testament times), while the rest of Revelation is apocalyptic literature. Our focus in this study will be on the messages to those seven churches and how that information is relevant for us today.

Selections for memorization. A Cuban pastor incarcerated in deplorable conditions for his faith told my friend afterward, "The Word of God was of great comfort. One Methodist pastor took a notebook and a pencil and wrote down all the Scriptures that everyone knew by heart and recorded them for all of us to read the Word of God." In the absence of Bibles, the only access these prisoners had to God's Word was what they'd hidden in their hearts—treasures their captors could never take away. Whether we live where Christians endure horrific persecution or we can worship freely but are tempted by materialism's pull, we need God's Word in our hearts to help us stand strong in every situation. So each week you'll find verses to memorize.

Are you ready for our trip through ancient Turkey to the seven churches in the Book of Revelation? If so, fasten your seat belt and travel back in time with us to the ancient world, where our journey begins.

INTRODUCTION TO
SUMATRA WITH THE SEVEN
CHURCHES

The chapters we will explore in *Sumatra with the Seven Churches* differ significantly from the rest of the Book of Revelation. The section we will consider contains messages from Christ to seven first-century churches in Asia Minor, while the rest of Revelation is apocalyptic (end-of-the-world) literature. Our focus in this study will be on the messages to those seven churches and how that information is relevant for us.

Because these churches have so much in common with where we live today, we can learn much from Jesus' expressed desires for them. Beginning with week 2 as you move through this study, you will complete a portion of the chart on pages xii–xiii to summarize what you learn.

The book. The title of the book of the Bible that contains the passage we'll explore is the Book of Revelation. Notice that *Revelation* is singular, not plural. Though the Book of Revelation contains a number of visions, they make up one grand revelation.

The author. The writer of the Book of Revelation refers to himself as John (1:1, 4, 9; 22:8). He adds no further information about his identity, which means either his readers personally knew him well or his reputation preceded him.

We find the name John attached with a number of books of the Bible. John the apostle, the brother of James and one of the sons of Zebedee, probably wrote the Gospel of John. And someone by the name of John clearly wrote the epistles of 1 John, 2 John, and 3 John. The apostle John may have written them all. Yet assuming the same person wrote them all in addition to Revelation might be a little like assuming Mary of Bethany and Mary Magdalene were the same—a mistake the church made for centuries. The author of Revelation refers to the "twelve apostles of the Lamb" (Rev. 21:14) without including himself in that group. So we might think John the apostle couldn't have been among them. Yet John the apostle, writer of the Gospel of John, maintained the same level of anonymity in that book.

In his classic commentary on the whole Bible, Matthew Henry observes that in the Old Testament's historical books, the authors are not always identified (for example, Judges, Ruth, and Chronicles), while the prophetic books always include the name of the one delivering God's message (for example, Isaiah, Micah, and Ezekiel). The same appears to be the case in the New Testament, where writers recording history (in the Gospels and Acts) didn't affix their names, but the one prophetic book—Revelation—includes the name of its scribe.

In the end we know only that someone named John recorded the vision, and tradition says it was either John the apostle or possibly a different John called "the elder." But here's what we do know: the original message-giver in the Book of Revelation, the one whose words John dictated, was Jesus Christ.

Still, the text does give us some hints about John's identity. We know from his word choice in several places that he was probably a Palestinian Jew. He leaves hints that Greek was his second language, his first probably being Hebrew or Aramaic. Many Jews had to flee Palestine following the revolt of AD 66–73, so John may have been one of those who fled to Asia Minor as a refugee.

> A number of DVD series on the Roman Empire provide background on what the world was like at the time John received his vision—around AD 90. Check out one or several to give yourself a context for the times.

The place. When the Lord appeared to John in a vision, he was on the Greek volcanic island of Patmos, which lies close to Turkey in the Aegean Sea. It is the northernmost of the *Dodecanese* ("twelve islands") group. Named

MAP OF THE SEVEN CHURCHES OF REVELATION
(LOCATED IN MODERN-DAY TURKEY)

for palms that used to cover the island,[1] Patmos is small, dry, and sea-horse-shaped, about ten miles long and six miles wide. Tradition says the Romans sent John into exile on Patmos for his faith and that he worked in mines and lived in a cave (that pilgrims still visit). The island lies off the coast of Miletus, near Ephesus, the first of the seven churches of Revelation. Eusebius recorded that when Nerva succeeded Domitian as emperor, John left the island and chose Ephesus for his home.

The time. Two thousand years ago Rome ruled the world—from present-day England to Africa, Syria to Spain. In those days one in every four people on earth lived under Roman law.

At the top of the social and political ladder stood the emperor. From the time of Caesar Augustus until AD 90, when John probably wrote Revelation, despite a few good or even great emperors, most abused power. Many, including Domitian, had reigns of brutality.

---

[1] Charles L. Souvay, "Patmos," The Original Catholic Encyclopedia, <http://oce.catholic.com/index.php?title=Patmos> accessed May 25, 2009.

Synopsis of Revelation 2 and 3					
Church	Description of Jesus Christ	Commendation	Criticism	Exhortation	Promise to Conquerors
Ephesus (2:1–7)					
Smyrna (2:8–11)					
Pergamum (2:12–17)					
Thyatira (2:18–29)					

Synopsis of Revelation 2 and 3

Church	Description of Jesus Christ	Commendation	Criticism	Exhortation	Promise to Conquerors
Sardis (3:1–6)					
Philadelphia (3:7–13)					
Laodicea (3:14–22)					

Nine years before John wrote, the emperor Titus died of a fever—or perhaps his doctor poisoned him, constrained by Titus's brother, Domitian. At that time the Roman Senate declared Titus a god, and Domitian succeeded him. Iranaeus, a church father born in Asia Minor who wrote in the second century, recorded that John received his vision "toward the end of Domitian's reign."[2] Domitian continued his rule of violence about six more years, until his wife and enemies finally murdered him.

Emperors in order from the time of Christ until AD 90, when John wrote Revelation: Augustus, Tiberius, Caligula, Claudius, Nero, year of the four emperors, Vespasian, Titus, Domitian

In a world filled with violence and volatile leaders, John provided a glimpse of the earth's true Ruler, who will return on a white horse and reign in justice and righteousness. John's record of his visions was the last book of the Bible to be written and closes out the New Testament.

[2] Irenaeus. *Adv. Haer.* 5.30.3

CONTENTS

WEEK 1 OF 8

You've Got Mail: Revelation 1

SUNDAY: THE MAIN THING

Scripture: "Look! He is returning with the clouds, and every eye will see him, even those who pierced him, and all the tribes on the earth will mourn because of him. This will certainly come to pass! Amen" (Rev. 1:7).

Think for a moment about the different letters you receive. A thank-you note. A notification of bad news. A postcard bringing greetings from another continent. A past-due notice. A shower invitation.

Think too of the ways we communicate with each other. Snail mail. Twitter. Blogs. E-mail. Youtube. Texting. Scribbling a note and posting it somewhere. Using the telephone.

Two thousand years ago when God wanted to communicate, he often did so through visions while people were awake or through dreams while they were asleep. So when Jesus wanted to communicate messages to seven churches in Asia Minor, he appeared to John—perhaps their overseer—in a vision. And John saw some amazing things to come.

1

Jesus told John to record what he saw, and as a result we have the Book of Revelation. In this study we will explore only the part of the book comprised of letters to the seven churches. Still, it helps to begin with an overview of the entire Book of Revelation so we understand the setting in which the letters appear.

Revelation begins with a vision of the high and exalted Christ. Once the Revealer provides a glimpse of his glory, he instructs John through twenty-two separate visions. And in the beginning of those visions, John receives seven messages to give to seven literal churches.

Many who study the seven letters identify seven corresponding periods of church history, concluding that we are now in the Laodicean or last period. We have chosen not to approach the text this way, which would limit our view to only the final message. Instead, we will consider each of the seven letters as having much to teach us. In effect the churches' mail is our mail, because the words spoken to Christ-followers in the distant past provide timeless instruction that's still relevant.

The overall structure of Revelation is this: First, Jesus appears. Then he gives messages to the churches. After that we find a vision of the Judge and his judgments. Then we have a vision of the coming King, followed by a picture of the coming kingdom.

The seven letters to the churches are really postcard-length messages, and they differ from most of Revelation in that they consist of straight prose while the rest is apocalyptic. Each letter includes most or all of the following elements: a description of Jesus Christ, a commendation, an exhortation, a criticism, and a promise to those who overcome. Though Jesus directed his messages to these specific churches, we can read their mail and learn about what's important to him. We see what he rebukes, exhorts, commends, and blesses, and we find application for our own time.

The main focus of the letters and the entire vision is that Jesus will most certainly return, and he will do so unexpectedly, so his followers must be ready at any moment.

To the weary who are persevering, he brings reward and relief. To those living only for themselves, he brings judgment. Today we often hear about Jesus being our buddy, our friend, and our pal, yet while Christ does love and have compassion for his children, that is not the whole picture. He is also the Almighty, the all-knowing, the omnipresent King and Creator, to whom worship and obedience are due. He makes the mountains roar and the lightning flash. He is the

Ancient of Days, holy, righteous, and pure. When he judges, he will judge righteously because he, the impartial one, knows all and misunderstands nothing.

When you think of his coming, do you look forward to blessing and relief? Or does the stuff of earth compete with your desire to see him? Do you want to be married first, or have children first, or have grandchildren first, or finish something first? Are you living with only the here-and-now in view, or do you delight at the thought that at any moment you could see his face?

What needs to shift in your focus so your greatest desire is to see the face of Jesus Christ?

MONDAY: SEVEN LETTERS FOR SEVEN CHURCHES

1. Before taking an in-depth look at the specific messages, get an overview of the Spirit's message to the seven churches. Find a quiet place, pray for insight, and read aloud Revelation 1–3.

Revelation 1

1:1 "The revelation of Jesus Christ, which God gave him to show his servants what must happen very soon. He made it clear by sending his angel to his servant John, **1:2** who then testified to everything that he saw concerning the word of God and the testimony about Jesus Christ. **1:3** Blessed is the one who reads the words of this prophecy aloud, and blessed are those who hear and obey the things written in it, because the time is near!

1:4 "From John, to the seven churches that are in the province of Asia: Grace and peace to you from 'he who is,' and who was, and who is still to come, and from the seven spirits who are before his throne, **1:5** and from Jesus Christ—the faithful witness, the first-born from among the dead, the ruler over the kings of the earth. To the one who loves us and has set us free from our sins at the cost of his own blood **1:6** and has appointed us as a kingdom, as priests serving his God and Father—to him be the glory and the power for ever and ever! Amen.

1:7 "(*Look! He is returning with the clouds,*
and every eye will see him,
even those who pierced him,
and all the tribes on the earth will mourn because of him.
This will certainly come to pass! Amen.)

1:8 "'I am the Alpha and the Omega,' says the Lord God—the one who is, and who was, and who is still to come—the All-Powerful!

1:9 "I, John, your brother and the one who shares with you in the persecution, kingdom, and endurance that are in Jesus, was on the island called Patmos because of the word of God and the testimony about Jesus. **1:10** I was in the Spirit on the Lord's Day when I heard behind me a loud voice like a trumpet, **1:11** saying: 'Write in a book what you see and send it to the seven churches—to Ephesus, Smyrna, Pergamum, Thyatira, Sardis, Philadelphia, and Laodicea.'

1:12 "I turned to see whose voice was speaking to me, and when I did so, I saw seven golden lampstands, **1:13** and in the midst of the lampstands was one like a son of man. He was dressed in a robe extending down to his feet and he wore a wide golden belt around his chest. **1:14** His head and hair were as white as wool, even as white as snow, and his eyes were like a fiery flame. **1:15** His feet were like polished bronze refined in a furnace, and his voice was like the roar of many waters. **1:16** He held seven stars in his right hand, and a sharp double-edged sword extended out of his mouth. His face shone like the sun shining at full strength. **1:17** When I saw him I fell down at his feet as though I were dead, but he placed his right hand on me and said: "Do not be afraid! I am the first and the last, **1:18** and the one who lives! I was dead, but look, now I am alive—forever and ever—and I hold the keys of death and of Hades! **1:19** Therefore write what you saw, what is, and what will be after these things. **1:20** The mystery of the seven stars that you saw in my right hand and the seven golden lampstands is this: The seven stars are the angels of the seven churches and the seven lampstands are the seven churches.

Seven Churches of Revelation Rediscovered
(DVD, 1999)
A forty-minute documentary features host David Nunn as he takes viewers to Turkey to the seven cities of Revelation 2–3. Nunn points out the unique attributes—such as aqueducts or eye salve—of these locations, providing information that helps viewers better understand the context for each of the Lord's seven messages.

Revelation 2

2:1 "To the angel of the church in Ephesus, write the following:

"'This is the solemn pronouncement of the one who has a firm grasp on the seven stars in his right hand—the one who walks among the seven golden lampstands: **2:2** "I know your works as well as your labor and steadfast endurance, and that you cannot tolerate evil. You have even put to the test those who refer to themselves as apostles (but are not), and have discovered that they are false. **2:3** I am also aware that you have persisted steadfastly, endured much for the sake of my name, and have not grown weary. **2:4** But I have this against you: You have departed from your first love! **2:5** Therefore, remember from what high state you have fallen and repent! Do the deeds you did at the first; if not, I will come to you and remove your lampstand from its place—that is, if you do not repent. **2:6** But you do have this going for you: You hate what the Nicolaitans practice—practices I also hate. **2:7** The one who has an ear had better hear what the Spirit says to the churches. To the one who conquers, I will permit him to eat from the tree of life that is in the paradise of God."'

2:8 "To the angel of the church in Smyrna write the following:

"'This is the solemn pronouncement of the one who is the first and the last, the one who was dead, but came to life: **2:9** "I know the distress you are suffering and your poverty (but you are rich). I also know the slander against you by those who call themselves Jews and really are not, but are a synagogue of Satan. **2:10** Do not be afraid of the things you are about to suffer. The devil is about to have some of you thrown into prison so you may be tested, and you will experience suffering for ten days. Remain faithful even to the point of death, and I will give you the crown that is life itself. **2:11** The one who has an ear had better hear what the Spirit says to the churches. The one who conquers will in no way be harmed by the second death.'"

2:12 "To the angel of the church in Pergamum write the following:

"'This is the solemn pronouncement of the one who has the sharp double-edged sword: **2:13** "I know where you live—where Satan's throne is. Yet you continue to cling to my name and you have not denied your faith in me, even in the days of Antipas, my faithful witness, who was killed in your city where Satan lives. **2:14** But I have a few things against you: You have some people there who follow the teaching of Balaam, who instructed Balak to put a stumbling block before the people of Israel so they would eat food sacrificed to idols and commit sexual immorality. **2:15** In the same way, there are also some among you who follow the teaching of the Nicolaitans. **2:16** Therefore, repent! If not, I will come against you quickly and make war against those people with the sword of my mouth. **2:17** The one who has an ear had better hear what the Spirit says to the churches. To the one who conquers, I will give him some of the hidden manna, and I will give him a white stone, and on that stone will be written a new name that no one can understand except the one who receives it.'"

2:18 "To the angel of the church in Thyatira write the following:

"This is the solemn pronouncement of the Son of God, the one who has eyes like a fiery flame and whose feet are like polished bronze: **2:19** 'I know your deeds: your love, faith, service, and steadfast endurance. In fact, your more recent deeds are greater than your earlier ones. **2:20** But I have this against you: You tolerate that woman Jezebel, who calls herself a prophetess, and by her teaching deceives my servants to commit sexual immorality and to eat food sacrificed to idols. **2:21** I have given her time to repent, but she is not willing to repent of her sexual immorality. **2:22** Look! I am throwing her onto a bed of violent illness, and those who commit adultery with her into terrible suffering, unless they repent of her deeds. **2:23** Furthermore, I will strike her followers with a deadly disease, and then all the churches will know that I am the one who searches minds and hearts. I will repay each one of you what your deeds deserve. **2:24** But to the rest of you in Thyatira, all who do not hold to this teaching (who have not learned the so-called 'deep secrets of Satan'), to you I say: I do not put any additional burden on you. **2:25** However, hold on to what you have until I come. **2:26** And to the one who conquers and who continues in my deeds until the end, I will give him authority over the nations—

2:27 he will rule them with an iron rod and like clay jars he will break them to pieces,

2:28 just as I have received the right to rule from my Father— and I will give him the morning star. **2:29** The one who has an ear had better hear what the Spirit says to the churches.'"

Revelation 3

3:1 "To the angel of the church in Sardis write the following:

"This is the solemn pronouncement of the one who holds the seven spirits of God and the seven stars: 'I know your deeds, that you have a reputation that you are alive, but in reality you are dead. **3:2** Wake up then, and strengthen what remains that was about to die, because I have not found your deeds complete in the sight of my God. **3:3** Therefore, remember what you received and heard, and obey it, and repent. If you do not wake up, I will come like a thief, and you will never know at what hour I will come against you. **3:4** But you have a few individuals in Sardis who have not stained their clothes, and they will walk with me dressed in white, because they are worthy. **3:5** The one who conquers will be dressed like them in white clothing, and I will never erase his name from the book of life, but will declare his name before my Father and before his angels. **3:6** The one who has an ear had better hear what the Spirit says to the churches.'

3:7 "To the angel of the church in Philadelphia write the following:

"This is the solemn pronouncement of the Holy One, the True One, who holds the key of David, who opens doors no one can shut, and shuts doors no one can open: **3:8** 'I know your deeds. (Look! I have put in front of you an open door that no one can shut.) I know that you have little strength, but you have obeyed my word and have not denied my name. **3:9** Listen! I am going to make those people from the synagogue of Satan—who say they are Jews yet are not, but are lying—Look, I will make them come and bow down at your feet and acknowledge that I have loved you. **3:10** Because you have kept my admonition to endure steadfastly, I will also keep you from the hour of testing that is about to come on the whole world to test those who live on the earth. **3:11** I am coming soon. Hold on to what you have so that no one can take away your crown. **3:12** The one who conquers I will make a pillar in the temple of my God, and he will never depart from it. I will write on him the name of my God and the name of the city of my God (the new Jerusalem that comes down out of heaven from my God), and my new name as well. **3:13** The one who has an ear had better hear what the Spirit says to the churches.'

3:14 "To the angel of the church in Laodicea write the following:

"This is the solemn pronouncement of the Amen, the faithful and true witness, the originator of God's creation: **3:15** "I know your deeds, that you are neither cold nor hot. I wish you were either cold or hot! **3:16** So because you are lukewarm, and neither hot nor cold, I am going to vomit you out of my mouth! **3:17** Because you say, 'I am rich and have acquired great wealth, and need nothing,' but do not realize that you are wretched, pitiful, poor, blind, and naked, **3:18** take my advice and buy gold from me refined by fire so you can become rich! Buy from me white clothing so you can be clothed and your shameful nakedness will not be exposed, and buy eye salve to put on your eyes so you can see! **3:19** All those I love, I rebuke and discipline. So be earnest and repent! **3:20** Listen! I am standing at the door and knocking! If anyone hears my voice and opens the door I will come into his home and share a meal with him, and he with me. **3:21** I will grant the one who conquers permission to sit with me on my throne, just as I too conquered and sat down with my Father on his throne. **3:22** The one who has an ear had better hear what the Spirit says to the churches."'"

2. What ideas, commands, or truths stood out to you as you read?

_____

_____

TUESDAY: THE AUTHOR AND HIS MESSAGE

1. Note how the author identifies himself four times in Revelation 1–2.

1:1 "The revelation of Jesus Christ, which God gave him to show his servants what must happen very soon. He made it clear by sending his angel to his servant John."

1:4 "From John, to the seven churches that are in the province of Asia: Grace and peace to you from 'he who is,' and who was, and who is still to come, and from the seven spirits who are before his throne.,"

1:9 "I, John, your brother and the one who shares with you in the persecution, kingdom, and endurance that are in Jesus, was on the island called Patmos because of the word of God and the testimony about Jesus. **1:10** I was in the Spirit on the Lord's Day when I heard behind me a loud voice like a trumpet, **1:11** saying: 'Write in a book what you see and send it to the seven churches—to Ephesus, Smyrna, Pergamum, Thyatira, Sardis, Philadelphia, and Laodicea.'"

. . . .

22:8 "I, John, am the one who heard and saw these things, and when I heard and saw them, I threw myself down to worship at the feet of the angel who was showing them to me."

Summarize how John describes himself.

_____

_____

- *The revelation* (1:1). *Revelation* identifies the book's subject. The word comes from the Greek *apokalypsis*, from which we derive *apocalypse*. Many think *apocalypse* means "disaster," but it actually refers to something that's "unveiled" or "uncovered." Like a beautiful veiled painting or statue, God's plan for the future is finally uncovered or revealed through this vision. He is the kind of Lord who reveals himself and his plans rather than keeping everything a secret.
- *Of Jesus Christ* (1:1). The phrase "of Jesus Christ" probably does not mean the revelation is *about* Jesus Christ, but rather what he reveals. In Greek as in English, *of* can indicate equivalency; for example, "the city of Philadelphia" means "the city that is Philadelphia." But *of* also can indicate possession or belonging—"a friend of mine" means "my friend." Here the phrase that follows, "which God gave him," tips the idea toward possession. We have the revelation *belonging* to Jesus Christ, which the Father gave him. Christ is seen in this book as the exalted Lord.

2. As you read Revelation 1:1–6 identify the personalities listed in the chain of communication for this revelation (for example, God —> Jesus —>Angel).

> **1:1** "The revelation of Jesus Christ, which God gave him to show his servants what must happen very soon. He made it clear by sending his angel to his servant John, **1:2** who then testified to everything that he saw concerning the word of God and the testimony about Jesus Christ. **1:3** Blessed is the one who reads the words of this prophecy aloud, and blessed are those who hear and obey the things written in it, because the time is near!"
>
> **1:4** "From John, to the seven churches that are in the province of Asia: Grace and peace to you from 'he who is,' and who was, and who is still to come, and from the seven spirits who are before his throne, **1:5** and from Jesus Christ—the faithful witness, the firstborn from among the dead, the ruler over the kings of the earth. To the one who loves us and has set us free from our sins at the cost of his own blood **1:6** and has appointed us as a kingdom, as priests serving his God and Father—to him be the glory and the power for ever and ever! Amen."

List the personalities here.

_____

_____

3. For what purpose was the revelation given, according to Revelation 1:1?

_____

_____

• *What must happen very soon* (1:1). The word *soon* appears seven times in Revelation (see also 2:16; 3:11; 11:14; 22:7, 12, 20). The focus in these contexts is not necessarily on immediacy in a chronological sense, but rather on suddenness. For some the idea that Jesus is coming suddenly brings joy; for others it evokes fear and serves as a warning. Jesus could return at any moment!

_____

_____

• *By sending his angel* (1:1). The word for *angel* and for *messenger* is the same in Koine Greek, the language in which the New Testament was written. Only context tells us which way to translate it. Here the messenger or angel bringing the vision remains unnamed, but because Gabriel announced messages to Daniel, Mary, and Zechariah, many believe Gabriel is the one bringing Jesus' revelation to John.
• *To his servant* (1:1). The word John uses to describe himself is *doulos,* which we could also translate "slave." We find it frequently at the beginning of biblical epistles (see Rom. 1:1; Phil. 1:1; Titus 1:1; James 1:1; 2 Peter 1:1; Jude 1). Notice the humility expressed in this word. In fact, apostles, prophets, and teachers in the first-century church did not refer to themselves as rulers, leaders, or masters. They called themselves servants or slaves of Christ. (What a lesson to those of us who lead! We may not mind serving others, but we certainly don't like being *treated* like slaves.)

4. What was John's response to the revelation (v. 2)?

_____

_____

5. What should be the reader's response to Jesus' revelation and why (v. 3)?

_____

_____

Which is the most difficult for you and why?

_____

_____

6. According to Revelation 1:3, who is blessed and why?

_____

_____

• *The time is near* (1:3). Hearers need to listen and heed because the time (*kairos*) of crisis is near. The word for *time* here is not the one referring to chronological time (*chronos*) but the one referring to opportunity or the right season. This word combined with the earlier time reference, "soon," adds to the urgency. Sometimes in biblical prophetic utterances like this, the word *time* refers specifically to end-time events. Remember when Jesus' disciples asked him about future events? He told them it was not for them to know the times (same word) or the periods (Acts 1:7).

7. The angel told John (1:3) that "the time is near." Yet we are still waiting today to see the prophecy in Revelation fulfilled. How would you explain this to someone who is skeptical, and what Scripture would you use to support your answer? As you think about your response, consider another passage:

2 Peter 3:8 "Now, dear friends, do not let this one thing escape your notice, that a single day is like a thousand years with the Lord and a thousand years are like a single day. **3:9** The Lord is not slow concerning his promise, as some regard slowness, but is being patient toward you, because he does not wish for any to perish but for all to come to repentance. **3:10** But the day of the Lord will come like a thief; when it comes, the heavens will disappear with a horrific noise, and the celestial bodies will melt away in a blaze, and the earth and every deed done on it will be laid bare."

---

8. Revelation 1:3 is the first of seven beatitudes in the book. These begin with the word *blessed*, which means much more than "happy." *Blessed* focuses more on being in right relationship with God than on great circumstances. Think of Paul and Silas singing while imprisoned in a dank, unlit Philippian jail hole. Their circumstances stunk, yet they offered praise to God (see Acts 16:25). Read this list of the beatitudes found in Revelation:

1:3 "Blessed is the one who reads the words of this prophecy aloud, and blessed are those who hear and obey the things written in it, because the time is near!"

14:13 "Then I heard a voice from heaven say, 'Write this: "Blessed are the dead, those who die in the Lord from this moment on!"'

"'Yes,' says the Spirit, 'so they can rest from their hard work, because their deeds will follow them.'"

16:15 "(Look! I will come like a thief! Blessed is the one who stays alert and does not lose his clothes so that he will not have to walk around naked and his shameful condition be seen.)"

19:9 "Then the angel said to me, 'Write the following: Blessed are those who are invited to the banquet at the wedding celebration of the Lamb!' He also said to me, 'These are the true words of God.'"

20:6 "Blessed and holy is the one who takes part in the first resurrection. The second death has no power over them, but they will be priests of God and of Christ, and they will reign with him for a thousand years."

22:7 "Look! I am coming soon! Blessed is the one who keeps the words of the prophecy expressed in this book."

22:14 "Blessed are those who wash their robes so they can have access to the tree of life and can enter into the city by the gates."

9. Summarize who is blessed in these passages and indicate the reason.
   Who is blessed   Why

_____

_____

_____

_____

_____

_____

10. We don't know the exact day Jesus will return, but God's Word tells us he will. If you knew Jesus would return today, how would you spend your remaining time on earth? Do you have relationships you need to reconcile, wrongs to right, people with whom you need to share Christ? List them and then spend some time in repentance and prayer.

_____

_____

WEDNESDAY: CHRIST EXALTED

1. Pray for insight; then read aloud Revelation 1:4–16.

1:4 "From John, to the seven churches that are in the province of Asia: Grace and peace to you from 'he who is,' and who was, and who is still to come, and from the seven spirits who are before his throne, **1:5** and from Jesus Christ—the faithful witness, the first-born from among the dead, the ruler over the kings of the earth. To the one who loves us and has set us free from our sins at the cost of his own blood **1:6** and has appointed us as a kingdom, as priests serving his God and Father—to him be the glory and the power for ever and ever! Amen."

The original audience hearing Revelation was not necessarily literate, and the message was intended to be read aloud in a group. Consider obtaining an audio version of Revelation and listening to it.

1:7 (Look! *He is returning with the clouds,* and *every eye will see him,*

even those who pierced him,

and *all the tribes on the earth will mourn because of him.*

This will certainly come to pass! Amen.)

1:8 "I am the Alpha and the Omega," says the Lord God—the one who is, and who was, and who is still to come—the All-Powerful!

1:9 "I, John, your brother and the one who shares with you in the persecution, kingdom, and endurance that are in Jesus, was on the island called Patmos because of the word of God and the testimony about Jesus. **1:10** I was in the Spirit on the Lord's Day when I heard behind me a loud voice like a trumpet, **1:11** saying: 'Write in a book what you see and send it to the seven churches—to Ephesus, Smyrna, Pergamum, Thyatira, Sardis, Philadelphia, and Laodicea.'

1:12 "I turned to see whose voice was speaking to me, and when I did so, I saw seven golden lampstands, **1:13** and in the midst of the lampstands was one like a son of man. He was dressed in a robe extending down to his feet and he wore a wide golden belt around his chest. **1:14** His head and hair were as white as wool, even as white as snow, and his eyes were like a fiery flame. **1:15** His feet were like polished bronze refined in a furnace, and his voice was like the roar of many waters. **1:16** He held seven stars in his right hand, and a sharp double-edged sword extended out of his mouth. His face shone like the sun shining at full strength."

2. John identifies his recipients, who are possibly congregations over which he has oversight. They all live within roughly two hundred miles of each other. According to Revelation 1:4, 11, who are they?

_____

_____

- *Grace and peace* (1:4). A common New Testament greeting, "grace and peace" combines a slight variation on the Greek *grace* with the Hebrew *peace* to pronounce blessing on Jewish and Gentile believers who are united as one in Christ. In some ways it's like saying "Aloha, y'all" to a group of Christians from Hawaii and Texas.

- *"He who is," and who was, and who is still to come* (1:4). This phrase is a variation on "who was and who is, and who is still to come!" (4:8). The phrase "he who is" appears within quotation marks because it is probably a reference to Exodus 3:14, where God described himself to Moses as "I AM." The third-person way to say that is "he is."

> To acquaint yourself with the geography, find the sites of the seven churches of Revelation by locating these cities on Google Earth or a map. All are located in modern-day Turkey: Kuşadasi (Ephesus), Izmir (Smyrna), Bergama (Pergamum), Akhisar (near Thyatira), Sardes (Sardis), Philadelphia, and Laodikeia (Laodicea).

- *From the seven spirits before his throne* (1:4). Four times in Revelation we see reference to the seven spirits of God, who in this case partner with Jesus in sending grace. Notice the word *seven* appears twelve times between Revelation 1:4 and 2:1 (emphasis added in bold below):

> **Revelation 1:4** "From John, to the **seven** churches . . . and from the **seven** spirits who are before his throne."
>
> **1:12** "I saw **seven** golden lampstands."
>
> **1:16** "He held **seven** stars in his right hand."
>
> **1:20** The mystery of the **seven** stars that you saw in my right hand and the **seven** golden lampstands is this: The **seven** stars are the angels of the **seven** churches and the **seven** lampstands are the **seven** churches."
>
> **2:1** "This is the solemn pronouncement of the one who has a firm grasp on the **seven** stars in his right hand—the one who walks among the **seven** golden lampstands.' "

Some think the reference to "seven spirits" here refers to characteristics of God (for example, a spirit of discernment, a spirit of wisdom, etc.). Consider this verse from Isaiah:

> **11:2** The Lord's spirit will rest on him –
> a spirit that gives extraordinary wisdom,
> a spirit that provides the ability to execute plans,
> a spirit that produces absolute loyalty to the Lord.

Another possibility is that the spirits before the throne are Christ's angel messengers. They appear before the throne and receive the word from the Lord for each of the churches. If so, it appears that each church or city has its own assigned angel.

3. What three titles does John ascribe to Jesus Christ in verse 5, and what is the significance of each title?

1:5 "And from Jesus Christ—the faithful witness, the firstborn from among the dead, the ruler over the kings of the earth."

_____

_____

• *The faithful witness* (1:5). In the Gospel of John, we read that Jesus was with God and Jesus was God. He has been witness through all time of the counsels and will of God, and all he says is true. His followers may depend on his Word as true in all things.

• *Firstborn from among the dead* (1:5). Jesus was Mary's firstborn son, but being firstborn over all creation or firstborn from the dead is altogether different from being chronologically first. Think of the phrase "first in the hearts of his countrymen," used to describe George Washington, to get a bit of the sense. *Firstborn* as it is used here of Jesus carries the idea of being preeminent. The fact that he is firstborn suggests others less eminent are coming after him whom God will also raise from the dead.

4. Knowing that *firstborn* means "preeminent," what do you think John means when he writes that Jesus is "firstborn from among the dead," and how—of all people in history—does this title uniquely describe Jesus?

_____

_____

• *Ruler over the kings of the earth* (1:5). Jesus is called King of kings and Lord of lords or vice versa in two other places in Revelation (17:14; 19:16). Imagine Alexander the Great, Julius Caesar, Mao Tsetung, Napoleon Bonaparte, Winston Churchill, George Washington,

Margaret Thatcher—imagine all the kings, presidents, emperors, and prime ministers ever to live. Picture them falling at Jesus' feet, obeying his command. He reigns in heaven as ruler of all the earth, and Revelation teaches that he will someday sit on a literal throne and reign over the literal nations as the Prince of Peace.

5. What three things does the text say Jesus has done for his followers (1:5–6)?

_____

_____

6. Notice the variety of references that refer to a priesthood in the verses that follow.

1 Peter 2:5 "To you yourselves, as living stones, are built up as a spiritual house to be a holy priesthood and to offer spiritual sacrifices that are acceptable to God through Jesus Christ."

1 Peter 2:9 "But you are *a chosen race, a royal priesthood, a holy nation, a people of his own,* so that you may *proclaim the virtues* of* the one who called you out of darkness into his marvelous light."

Revelation 5:10 "You have appointed them as a kingdom and priests to serve our God, and they will reign on the earth."

What do you think it means that Jesus has made us a kingdom and priests serving his God and Father?

_____

_____

_____

*Italics in the *NET Bible* indicate a reference to the Old Testament. Bold and italics mean a direct quotation from the Old Testament. In this case the reference is Exodus 19:6, which says, "'You will be to me a kingdom of priests and a holy nation.' These are the words that you will speak to the Israelites." Apparently God's initial desire was for all members of the nation of Israel to serve as priests. The ultimate function of a priest is to assist people in bringing offerings to God. Consider that in the original plan every person, male or female, was destined for priesthood. Following the resurrection of Christ, all believers are appointed as priests.

7. Many scholars consider Revelation 1:7 the key verse in Revelation:

> **1:7** *"Look! He is returning with the clouds, and every eye will see him, even those who pierced him,* and all the tribes on the earth will mourn because of him. This will certainly come to pass! Amen."

What promises do we find in this verse?

_____

_____

Who will see Jesus?

_____

_____

What will be their response?

_____

_____

Why do you think all the tribes on earth will mourn?

_____

_____

_____

8. The italics in Revelation 1:7 are there because the verse makes reference to a number of ancient predictions about the Messiah. Consider this one from the prophet Daniel:

> **Daniel 7:13** "I was watching in the night visions,
> And with the clouds of the sky
> one like a son of man was approaching.
> He went up to the Ancient of Days
> and was escorted before him.
> **7:14** To him was given ruling authority, honor, and
>   sovereignty.

All peoples, nations, and language groups were serving him.
His authority is eternal and will not pass away.
His kingdom will not be destroyed."

• *Amen* (1:7). The word *amen* appears seven times in Revelation, a number that, as mentioned earlier, occurs often. Seven is the number of completion or perfection. *Amen* means "truly" or "indeed." More casually, we might say, "This will come to pass. Definitely."

9. Summarize the characteristics (attributes) of God you find in today's passage. Which most encourages you today and why?

_____

_____

_____

10. Jesus refers to himself as "the Alpha and Omega . . . who is, and who was, and who is still to come—the All-Powerful!" (v. 8). Notice he doesn't say "was, is, and will be" as God is described elsewhere in the Bible. Why are these names and descriptions especially appropriate for the theme of a book that describes future events?

_____

_____

_____

• *Alpha and Omega* (1:8). Alpha and omega are the first and last letters of the Greek alphabet. The description of Christ as the first and last occurs three times in Revelation (1:8; 21:6; 22:13).
• *All-Powerful* (1:8).Of the ten times "all-powerful" appears in the New Testament, nine occur in Revelation (2 Cor. 6:18; Rev. 1:8; 4:8; 11:17; 15:3; 16:7, 14; 19:6, 15; 21:22). In this book of the Bible, we catch a glimpse of God as the almighty one. Before the messages to the churches, the hearers catch a glimpse of the ultimate evaluator who reigns.

11. Remember, John has probably been banished for his faith. Where was he when he received the revelation and what hint of persecution do you read in his reason for being there (1:9)?

_____

_____

12. What three things does John share in common with the believers receiving his message (v. 9), and what do you think it means to share in these things?

_____

_____

_____

13. In what ways have you shared in the "persecution, kingdom, and endurance" that are in Jesus (1:9)?

_____

_____

_____

14. Which attributes of God does John's description of Christ emphasize (1:12–16)?

_____

_____

• *A son of man* (1:13). We find the phrase "son of man" throughout the Bible. Often the phrase refers to humanity in general. But in the books of Ezekiel and Daniel, we find constant references to each of the prophets in these books as a "son of man" told to warn Israel of coming judgment. In one such instance, though, we find "son of man" as a reference to the coming Messiah:

Daniel 7:13 "I was watching in the night visions, 'And with the clouds of the sky one like a son of man was approaching. He went up to the Ancient of Days and was escorted before him. To him was given ruling authority, honor, and sovereignty. All peoples, nations, and language groups were serving him. His authority is eternal and will not pass away. His kingdom will not be destroyed.'"

Then in the Gospels, Jesus uses the title Son of Man to refer to himself. And when Stephen was dying as the crowd stoned him, he saw heaven open and the Son of Man standing at the right hand of God (Acts 7:56).

- *A wide golden belt around his chest* (1:13). The New American Standard Bible (NASB) renders this, "girded about the chest with a golden band." We don't usually use the word "girded" these days, yet knowing "girdles" were worn around the chest rather than the abdomen can help us better understand that soldiers, prophets, and priests in Old Testament times wore girdles of leather or fine linen. The sorrowing wore girdles of sackcloth. What does it say to you that Jesus is girded with a golden band/band of gold?
- *As the roar of many waters* (1:15). Have you ever heard the roar of the ocean? Or stood at Niagara Falls? John heard Jesus speak with volume and power.

John's readers would have been aware that at Rhodes, another island in the Aegean near Patmos, stood a monstrous statue dedicated to the god Helios (Greek for "sun"). This statue was sometimes included on ancient lists as one of the Seven Wonders of the Ancient World. People came from all over the empire to view this shining bronze colossus that stood 104 feet high holding a lamp. Its metal could fill nine hundred camel loads, and even the largest ship with sails spread full could glide under it to enter the inner harbor. Though an earthquake destroyed the statue in 223 BC, the Romans restored it.

Picture John's readers imagining this statue as they read a description of Jesus Christ. This image of the true God totally dwarfs any manmade colossus:

Revelation 1:13 "And in the midst of the lampstands was one like a son of man. He was dressed in a robe extending down to his feet and he wore a wide golden belt around his chest. **1:14** His head and hair were as white as wool, even as white as snow, and his eyes were like a fiery flame. **1:15** His feet were like polished bronze refined in a furnace, and his voice was like the roar of many waters. **1:16** He held seven stars in his right hand, and a sharp double-edged sword extended out of his mouth. His face shone like the sun shining at full strength."

16. Write out a prayer of worship in response to the description of Jesus Christ found in today's passage from Revelation.

You can find at least three DVDs available that explore the Seven Wonders of the Ancient World, such as the History Channel's "Ancient Mysteries" documentary on the subject. Consider ordering one and viewing the segment about the Colossus of Rhodes and the Temple of Ephesus.

_____

_____

THURSDAY: SHOCK AND AWE

1. Pray for insight; then read aloud Revelation 1:17–20.

> **1:17** "When I saw him I fell down at his feet as though I were dead, but he placed his right hand on me and said: 'Do not be afraid! I am the first and the last, **1:18** and the one who lives! I was dead, but look, now I am alive—forever and ever—and I hold the keys of death and of Hades! **1:19** Therefore write what you saw, what is, and what will be after these things. **1:20** The mystery of the seven stars that you saw in my right hand and the seven golden lampstands is this: The seven stars are the angels of the seven churches and the seven lampstands are the seven churches.'"

2. What was John's response to the vision (v. 17)?

_____

_____

3. What are some possible reasons John had this response?

_____

_____

4. Which attributes of God does Jesus' description of himself highlight?

_____

_____

5. What do you think Jesus means when he says he holds "the keys of death and of Hades" (v. 18)?

_____

_____

6. Often the Bible's visionary literature interprets itself, as is the case here. So in trying to figure out apocalyptic imagery, the place to start is in any explanations given in the immediate context, and then in finding similar imagery elsewhere in the Bible. For example, the Word of God is often referred to in the Bible as a sword, and in John's vision a sword comes out of Jesus' mouth. From our reading for this week we know that John saw stars and lampstands. According to verse 20, what do the seven lampstands and the seven stars represent?

_____

_____

7. What causes you to fear God or to fall before him?

_____

_____

8. What does the fact that Christ is the first and the last, the living One, alive forevermore, and holding the keys of death and Hades mean in terms of the church's needs and our own daily problems?

_____

_____

_____

9. The number seven occurs fifty-four times in the Book of Revelation. As mentioned earlier, in the Bible, seven is associated with completion, fulfillment, and perfection.[3] What do the following verses tell you about the association of the number seven with the idea of completion?

> **Genesis 2:2** "By the seventh day God finished the work that he had been doing, and he ceased on the seventh day all the work that he had been doing."

> **Exodus 20:8** "Remember the Sabbath day to set it apart as holy. **20:9** For six days you may labor and do all your work, **20:10** but the seventh day is a Sabbath to the Lord your God; on it you shall not do any work, you, or your son, or your daughter, or your male servant, or your female servant, or your cattle, or the resident foreigner who is in your gates. **20:11** For in six days the Lord made the heavens and the earth and the sea and all that is in them, and he rested on the seventh day; therefore the Lord blessed the Sabbath day and set it apart as holy."

> **Leviticus 14:7** "And sprinkle it seven times on the one being cleansed from the disease, pronounce him clean, and send the live bird away over the open countryside."

> **Acts 6:3** "But carefully select from among you, brothers, seven men who are well-attested, full of the Spirit and of wisdom, whom we may put in charge of this necessary task."

10. Take some time to reflect on your own view of Christ and your response to him. Do you have a holy, reverential awe for Jesus Christ? If not, why not?

---

[3] Charles Ryrie, The Ryrie Study Bible, Expanded Edition *(Chicago: Moody Press, 1995)*, 2013.

1. Reread aloud Revelation 1:

1:1 "The revelation of Jesus Christ, which God gave him to show his servants what must happen very soon. He made it clear by sending his angel to his servant John, **1:2** who then testified to everything that he saw concerning the word of God and the testimony about Jesus Christ. **1:3** Blessed is the one who reads the words of this prophecy aloud, and blessed are those who hear and obey the things written in it, because the time is near!"

1:4 "From John, to the seven churches that are in the province of Asia: Grace and peace to you from 'he who is,' and who was, and who is still to come, and from the seven spirits who are before his throne, **1:5** and from Jesus Christ—the faithful witness, the first-born from among the dead, the ruler over the kings of the earth. To the one who loves us and has set us free from our sins at the cost of his own blood **1:6** and has appointed us as a kingdom, as priests serving his God and Father—to him be the glory and the power for ever and ever! Amen.

1:7 "(Look! *He is returning with the clouds,*
and every eye will see him,
even those who pierced him,
and all the tribes on the earth will mourn because of him.
This will certainly come to pass! Amen.)

1:8 "'I am the Alpha and the Omega,' says the Lord God—the one who is, and who was, and who is still to come—the All-Powerful!

1:9 "I, John, your brother and the one who shares with you in the persecution, kingdom, and endurance that are in Jesus, was on the island called Patmos because of the word of God and the testimony about Jesus. **1:10** I was in the Spirit on the Lord's Day when I heard behind me a loud voice like a trumpet, **1:11** saying: 'Write in a book what you see and send it to the seven churches—to Ephesus, Smyrna, Pergamum, Thyatira, Sardis, Philadelphia, and Laodicea.'

1:12 "I turned to see whose voice was speaking to me, and when I did so, I saw seven golden lampstands, **1:13** and in the midst of the lampstands was one like a son of man. He was dressed in a robe extending down to his feet and he wore a wide golden belt around his chest. **1:14** His head and hair were as white as wool, even as white as snow, and his eyes were like a fiery flame. **1:15** His feet were like polished bronze refined in a furnace, and his voice was like the roar of many waters. **1:16** He held seven stars in his right hand, and a sharp double-edged sword extended out of his mouth. His face shone like the sun shining at full strength. **1:17** When I saw him I fell down at his feet as though I were dead, but he placed his right hand on me and said: "Do not be afraid! I am the first and the last, **1:18** and the one who lives! I was dead, but look, now I am alive—forever and ever—and I hold the keys of death and of Hades! **1:19** Therefore write what you saw, what is, and what will be after these things. **1:20** The mystery of the seven stars that you saw in my right hand and the seven golden lampstands is this: The seven stars are the angels of the seven churches and the seven lampstands are the seven churches."

2. Revelation 1 contains a lot of teaching (*doctrine*) about God and his ways. What do you see concerning each doctrine in the following verses?

Of salvation or *soteriology* (vv. 5–6)

_____

_____

Of Christ or *Christology* (vv. 5, 8, 17–18)

_____

_____

Of end times or *eschatology* (vv. 1, 3, 7)

_____

_____

3. If the Spirit of the King of kings and ruler of the universe is your returning master, what difference will it make in your life?

_____

_____

4. Have you placed your faith in the One who died and rose? Write a few sentences describing your best recollection of that experience.

_____

_____

5. In your own words describe the God you serve.

_____

_____

6. Read Peter's description of the coming "day of the Lord":

> **2 Peter 3:8** "Now, dear friends, do not let this one thing escape your notice, that a single day is like a thousand years with the Lord and a thousand years are like a single day. **3:9** The Lord is not slow concerning his promise, as some regard slowness, but is being patient toward you, because he does not wish for any to perish but for all to come to repentance. **3:10** But the day of the Lord will come like a thief; when it comes, the heavens will disappear with a horrific noise, and the celestial bodies will melt away in a blaze, and the earth and every deed done on it will be laid bare. **3:11** Since all these things are to melt away in this manner, what sort of people must we be, conducting our lives in holiness and godliness, **3:12** while waiting for and hastening the coming of the day of God? Because of this day, the heavens will be burned up and dissolve, and the celestial bodies will melt away in a blaze! **3:13** But, according to his promise, we are waiting for new heavens and a new earth, in which righteousness truly resides.
>
> **3:14** "Therefore, dear friends, since you are waiting for these things, strive to be found at peace, without spot or blemish, when you come into his presence. **3:15** And regard the patience of our Lord as salvation, just as also our dear brother Paul wrote to you, according to the wisdom given to him . . ."

In a well researched monograph, *Dress and the Roman Woman: Self-Presentation and Society*, Kelly Olson tells readers that yellow was the Roman woman's "pink." And while we may envision Romans wrapped in white, they actually loved color. And they also liked cosmetics. Yet lips were no big deal. To a Roman, skin was the thing. A beautiful complexion free of pockmarks or wrinkles would have been difficult to maintain in the ancient world. Think of what poor sanitation and diet, not to mention harsh skin treatments, disease, and the lack of acne aids would have done to devastate the face. Lighter skin was more highly valued, perhaps because wealthier people spent less time in the sun. So women used white lead to lighten up their faces. And that stuff can ravage the face. With that in mind, we read the description of how God wants us to be—"without spot or blemish." He's using the metaphor of an unwrinkled, perfect-skinned face to focus readers on the beauty God values, the moral perfection of an upright life.

7. Describe the coming "day of the Lord."

_____

_____

8. What does Peter exhort his readers to do in view of the Lord's return (v. 14–15)?

_____

_____

Sometimes people are fascinated with the Book of Revelation because it has so much symbolism. Yet while it is good to understand and recognize interesting spiritual truth, if we don't apply it to our lives, it is just head knowledge. As William Newell wrote in *The Book of Revelation*, "It will be vain to become occupied with 'sevens,' 'hundred-forty-four-thousands,' 'six-sixty-sixes,' the restoration of the Roman Empire, the person of the antichrist, the two wild beasts, the 'millennium,' or even the new Jerusalem, unless, along with God the Father, who has subjected all things unto *Him, Christ* is ever before our eyes!"[4]

[4] *William R. Newell*, The Book of the Revelation *(Chicago: Moody Press, 1935), 31.*

9. What similarities do you see between Peter's words and the message in Revelation 1?

_____

_____

_____

10. The greatness of Christ and the difference he makes in the world and in our lives is the reason we have spent much of this week worshipping him. Is your focus on him more than anyone or anything else? If not, why not? What needs to change in your priorities?

_____

_____

_____

SATURDAY: BRIGHTNESS OF THE SON

As I write this, I am sitting on a boat crossing the Aegean Sea, sailing from Patmos to Corinth. Though I didn't plan to, I awoke early enough this morning to catch the sunrise. Before it peeked over the mountains, the sky was cast in pink, yellow, and blue over indigo waters. Glorious! But once the sun emerged on the horizon, I had to stop pointing my camera directly toward the light, because the brilliance reflecting in my lens produced an overpowering glare.

My photo excursion complete, I grabbed a cup of coffee and my Bible and headed for a lawn chair on the deck. Our group of pilgrims had just seen Patmos and visited the cave where tradition says John received the revelation from Jesus. So I opened the biblical text and reread Revelation 1. Yet I ran into a bit of a challenge with reading, because I had only one hand free for holding my Bible open in the wind. I needed the other to shield my eyes as I cowered under the sun's piercing rays. I was squinting and turning my face away when my eyes fell on these words: "His face shone like the sun shining at full strength" (1:16).

Have you ever looked directly into the sun? If you have, I hope you've looked away quickly! Our eyes cannot endure it in all its strength. And the experience I've just described brought me face-to-face with three important characteristics of Jesus found in Revelation 1.

Jesus is glorious. Imagine John in a dark cave when suddenly Jesus appeared. John would have had to throw his hands over his eyes to shield them from the full-strength light. John tells his readers how he responded—he fell at Jesus' feet. It's as if John was so overcome that he passed out—"as though I were dead." John recognized his unworthiness in the face of the Lord's glorious, shining presence.

If the John of Revelation is the same John who accompanied Jesus during his earthly ministry, he had seen this glory once before. Matthew records what Peter, James, and John witnessed as Jesus was transfigured before them. There, as in Revelation, Jesus' face shone like the sun (Matt. 17:2).

John fell as if dead because he was terrified. And in response Jesus told him: "Do not be afraid"—the same words that shining angels spoke to frightened shepherds on a Judean hillside (Luke 2:10). Jesus' glory and his encouragement not to fear, however, were followed by a self-pronouncement from the Son of God about who he is: the Alpha and Omega. The one who rose from the dead.

Jesus is risen. In Revelation 4 we find a chronological view of Almighty God as the one who was and is and is to come—past, present, and future. In Revelation 1 we find a slightly different description. Here Jesus speaks of himself first as the one who *is,* then who was, and finally "who is still to come." Why would he change the order?

Reading on, we find Jesus emphasizes he is "the one who lives" and who "was dead" but is now alive. And not only that, he "was dead" but is "alive—forever and ever!" (1:18). All members of the Trinity have existed from eternity past. All are in the here and now. And all will exist forever. Yet the emphasis changes when Jesus describes himself: Jesus *is* because he is risen! A dead person "is" no longer. But Jesus *is* and was and is coming. And as the risen one, he "holds the keys of death and of Hades." The one who conquered death is master of it all. Everyone must ultimately die, but we worship the one who conquered death, and through him we have eternal life.

Jesus loves the church. And what is the desire of our glorious, risen Lord? In Revelation 1 we find him walking among the churches—not marble or wooden or concrete structures, but people redeemed and gathering in Jesus' name.

Our friend tells his son on Sunday mornings, "We are going to meet with the church in a building" rather than "We are going to church." He does this so his son will understand that the church is the people. And speaking about the seven churches, the people he loves, Jesus tells John that he has a firm grasp on them (see 1:16, 20; 2:1). The churches belong to his care and his control. He speaks to them because he cares about their welfare.

A major concern of Jesus Christ is the church, his bride. He wants her to emerge spotless when she is presented to him. So he commends her and challenges her and rebukes her so that she might be all she is supposed to be for the glory of the one who loves her.

Two thousand years later Jesus' concern for the church remains. We are "her."

Do you worship a glorious Lord? Do you believe he has all power over death—and in every lesser circumstance? Do you value the church for whom he died?

Ask God as you continue in this study to help you hear from him the commendations, admonitions, rebukes, and promises you need to become all that he desires you to be in Christ, your Lord, your Savior, your God.

Pray: Almighty God, who was and is and is to come, thank you for sending your Son who is and was and is coming suddenly. Thank you for his greatness and glory. Thank you that the Alpha and Omega rose from the dead and holds the keys of death and Hades. Thank you that you are almighty and that the Son of Man is in control. Thank you that you are glorious. Thank you that you love those ransomed with Jesus' blood. Search my heart that I might be ready at any moment for Jesus Christ's return, and grant me the courage and the love to tell others. Purify my heart for your glory and my good. In Jesus' name, Amen.

Memorize: "Look! *He is returning with the clouds, and every eye will see him, even those who pierced him,* and all the tribes on the earth will mourn because of him. This will certainly come to pass! Amen" (Rev. 1:7).

WEEK 2 OF 8

Ephesus: The Love-Lost Church
Revelation 2:1–7

Scripture: "This is the solemn pronouncement of the one who has a firm grasp on the seven stars in his right hand—the one who walks among the seven golden lampstands" (Rev. 2:1).

The first church in Revelation to receive Jesus' message was the church in Ephesus, which lay on the west coast of what we know as modern Turkey. The first time we find Ephesus mentioned in Scripture is Acts 18. Paul has left Corinth with the husband-and-wife team Aquila and Priscilla, and they all arrive in Ephesus. There Paul talks to Jews who urge him to tell them more, and Paul promises to return if the Lord wills. Then he heads to the interior to preach.

While Paul's gone, a man named Apollos comes to Ephesus and, although he is a wonderful orator, he doesn't know "the rest of the story" about Jesus. The last he heard was John the Baptizer's message. So Priscilla and Aquila take Apollos aside and teach him. Paul returns to Ephesus, and Acts 19:10 records that he stays there two years.

ACTS 19 RECORDS THAT THE PEOPLE OF EPHESUS YELLED "GREAT IS ARTEMIS OF THE EPHESIANS!" IN THIS THEATER FOR TWO HOURS.

Ephesus was a seaport and the capital of what they called Asia, but which we now refer to as Asia Minor. Today silt clogs the ancient harbor, requiring a seventeen-mile drive from the port at Kuşadasi. But in New Testament times, people from all over the empire sailed right up to the city port of Ephesus.

Even as people approached Ephesus from miles away, they could see the towering columns of Artemis's temple. Arguably the most magnificent of the Seven Wonders of the Ancient World, the mammoth structure stood more than four times the size of the Parthenon on the Acropolis in Athens. As we keep reading through Acts 19, we find that an uproar took place in Ephesus because Paul's gospel preaching threatened the trade of Artemis's silver workers.

So who was Artemis of the Ephesians? She was somewhat different from other manifestations of Artemis, in the same way that we might consider Black Barbie or Mermaid Barbie or Holiday Barbie the same but different from the blonde Barbie. According to Trebilco, a prominent Ephesus scholar, "It is often thought that

Artemis of Ephesus was a fertility goddess," yet this is probably incorrect.[5] In the same way midwives and obstetricians deal only with delivery and not necessarily fertility, Artemis was probably a deliverer-only goddess in Paul's day. In fact, ancient mythology includes a story of Artemis and Apollo shooting arrows through all the children of Niobe—Apollo killing the sons, and Artemis the daughters. So Artemis was no nurturing mother-goddess! And by New Testament times, we find no evidence of a fertility association. Women offered prayers to Artemis at their time of labor, pleading, "Deliver me safely or kill me quickly!" The name *Artemis* is derived from a word meaning *to save* or *be sound*.

So first-century pagans in Ephesus thought Artemis Ephesia saved or delivered, and she was deemed to have the power to deliver a first-century woman through the most dangerous of passages—childbirth. Though not a man hater or a radical feminist as we understand the term, Artemis was a confirmed virgin, and her cult leaders appear to have been sexually *in*active.

When Paul's gospel preaching threatened the trade of those who made silver idols of the goddess, a huge uproar ensued. Citizens poured into the theater that held (and still holds) more than twenty-five thousand people. They yelled for two hours, "Great is Artemis of the Ephesians!" The gospel threatened their livelihood.

Thirty or more years passed until John's vision included a message to the church in Ephesus. And tradition tells us that after writing this vision from Patmos, John settled in Ephesus.

Excavations in Ephesus over the past one hundred fifty years have revealed an amazing city with columned streets, an enormous theater, beautiful first-century homes preserved in a mudslide, and advanced water and drainage systems. Many people visit the now-uninhabited city and marvel at its opulent marble, fresco, and mosaic remains. And among the great works there lie numerous indications of the city's original commitment to the Greek pantheon and to the females in particular.

The Greek gods and goddesses were believed to inhabit only one place at a time; our God is omnipresent. The Greek gods and goddesses had limited knowledge; our God knows all. The gods and goddesses had limited powers; our God can do anything. Artemis—sometimes called Artemis Savior—might or might not save a woman in childbear-

[5] Trebilco, p. 23.

ing; our God, the Lord Jesus Christ, divine but flesh, entered time and space to serve and lay down his life that everyone who calls on the name of the Lord might be saved.

How great is our God!

·MONDAY: WOOLLY WOLVES

1. Knowing the prominence of the ancient city of Ephesus in New Testament history, you now have some background for the Lord's message to the Ephesians. Pray for insight from the Spirit; then read aloud the message from Christ to the church at Ephesus in Revelation 2:1–7:

> **Revelation 2:1** To the angel of the church in Ephesus, write the following:
>
> "This is the solemn pronouncement of the one who has a firm grasp on the seven stars in his right hand—the one who walks among the seven golden lampstands: **2:2** 'I know your works as well as your labor and steadfast endurance, and that you cannot tolerate evil. You have even put to the test those who refer to themselves as apostles (but are not), and have discovered that they are false. **2:3** I am also aware that you have persisted steadfastly, endured much for the sake of my name, and have not grown weary. **2:4** But I have this against you: You have departed from your first love! **2:5** Therefore, remember from what high state you have fallen and repent! Do the deeds you did at the first; if not, I will come to you and remove your lampstand from its place—that is, if you do not repent. **2:6** But you do have this going for you: You hate what the Nicolaitans practice—practices I also hate. **2:7** The one who has an ear had better hear what the Spirit says to the churches. To the one who conquers, I will permit him to eat from the tree of life that is in the paradise of God.'"

2 . In this message, what description of Jesus do you find?

_____

_____

_____

- If archeology interests you, check out the account of John Turtle Wood's discovery of the temple of Artemis when he was doing excavation for the British Museum in Ephesus more than a century ago. In his work *Discoveries at Ephesus*, Wood describes his Indiana Jones–like experiences. Another interesting work is *Ephesus: One Hundred Years of Excavation*, which includes extensive pictures and drawings about the ancient city near modern-day Kuşadasi, Turkey.
- You can see remains of the ancient city, including the theater described in Acts 19, by viewing it on Google Earth.
- Find out what ancient writers such as Strabo and Plutarch said about Ephesus in Jerome Murphy-O'Connor's book, *St. Paul's Ephesus: Texts and Archaeology* (Liturgical Press).
- For an outstanding exploration of Ephesus's biblical history, check out Paul Trebilco's *The Early Christians in Ephesus from Paul to Ignatius* (Eerdmans).

What commendation for the church?

_____

_____

What criticism?

_____

_____

What consequence and exhortation?

_____

_____

What promise to the one who conquers or the "overcomer"?

_____

_____

Use your answers to fill in the chart included at the beginning of this study.

1. Identify the location of Patmos and of Ephesus on the map at the beginning of this study.

2. Pray for insight; then read Revelation 2:1.

> **Revelation 2:1** "To the angel of the church in Ephesus, write the following:
>
> "This is the solemn pronouncement of the one who has a firm grasp on the seven stars in his right hand—the one who walks among the seven golden lampstands."

3. Think about how Jesus is described in Revelation 2:1. Considering that the seven golden lampstands are the churches, what does it mean that Jesus walks among them?

_____

_____

4. Read Paul's farewell address to the Ephesian elders at Miletus (Acts 20:25–32), which took place some forty-three years prior to John's revelation:

> **20:25** "And now I know that none of you among whom I went around proclaiming the kingdom will see me again. **20:26** Therefore I declare to you today that I am innocent of the blood of you all. **20:27** For I did not hold back from announcing to you the whole purpose of God. **20:28** Watch out for yourselves and for all the flock of which the Holy Spirit has made you overseers, to shepherd the church of God that he obtained with the blood of his own Son. **20:29** I know that after I am gone fierce wolves will come in among you, not sparing the flock. **20:30** Even from among your own group men will arise, teaching perversions of the truth to draw the disciples away after them. **20:31** Therefore be alert, remembering that night and day for three years I did not stop warning each one of you with tears. **20:32** And now I entrust you to God and to the

message of his grace. This message is able to build you up and give you an inheritance among all those who are sanctified."

What was Paul's greatest concern for the Ephesian church?

_____

_____

5. Read from Paul's instructions to Timothy in Ephesus recorded in 1 Timothy 1:3–7. What were some issues in and exhortations for the church of Ephesus that preceded the message to this church in Revelation?

> **1:3** "As I urged you when I was leaving for Macedonia, stay on in Ephesus to instruct certain people not to spread false teachings, **1:4** nor to occupy themselves with myths and interminable genealogies. Such things promote useless speculations rather than God's redemptive plan that operates by faith. **1:5** But the aim of our instruction is love that comes from a pure heart, a good conscience, and a sincere faith. **1:6** Some have strayed from these and turned away to empty discussion. **1:7** They want to be teachers of the law, but they do not understand what they are saying or the things they insist on so confidently."

_____

_____

6. According to these words of Paul, what characterized the false teachers?

_____

_____

7. What false teachings are prevalent in churches today?

_____

_____

8. How can we protect ourselves and our churches from being led astray by false doctrines and teachers?

_____

_____

9. Despite the risk of false teaching in the church, God is still in control of all that happens. He walks among the lampstands and holds the stars in his right hand. How have you seen his sovereign hand at work in your church and/or the body of Christ worldwide?

_____

_____

10. Read and summarize the following biblical warnings about and descriptions of false teachers:

> **Matthew 7:15–16** "Watch out for false prophets, who come to you in sheep's clothing but inwardly are voracious wolves. You will recognize them by their fruit. Grapes are not gathered from thorns or figs from thistles, are they?"

· ·

> **2 Corinthians 11:13–15** "For such people are false apostles, deceitful workers, disguising themselves as apostles of Christ. And no wonder, for even Satan disguises himself as an angel of light. Therefore it is not surprising his servants also disguise themselves as servants of righteousness, whose end will correspond to their actions."

· ·

> **2 John 7** "For many deceivers have gone out into the world, people who do not confess Jesus as Christ coming in the flesh. This person is the deceiver and the antichrist!"

11. Today false teachings still abound—the prosperity gospel, works-based salvation, doctrines that undermine the authority of God's Word. What steps can you take to inoculate yourself against false teaching?

_____

_____

12. What part can you play in "immunizing" others against false teaching?

_____

_____

13. Pray for yourself, your church, and for those in your faith community who need to grow in their understanding of Jesus Christ.

WEDNESDAY: COMMENDATIONS

1. Pray for the Spirit to grant insight; then read aloud Revelation 2:2–3, 6:

> **Revelation 2:2** "I know your works as well as your labor and steadfast endurance, and that you cannot tolerate evil. You have even put to the test those who refer to themselves as apostles (but are not), and have discovered that they are false. **2:3** I am also aware that you have persisted steadfastly, endured much for the sake of my name, and have not grown weary."
>
> **2:6** "But you do have this going for you: You hate what the Nicolaitans practice—practices I also hate."

2. For what was the church at Ephesus commended?

_____

_____

3. In light of Paul's farewell message to the elders of this church (which you read from Acts earlier in the week), how would you describe the Ephesian church through the years to this point?

_____

_____

_____

4. What does it mean that one "cannot tolerate evil" and why would that be considered a strength?

_____

_____

5. The church at Ephesus was commended for their perseverance and for not growing weary. How can you help others in your faith community to persevere and not grow weary?

_____

_____

6. What circumstances in your own life make you weary in your faith? List them and then pray over each one, asking God to give you strength to endure.

_____

_____

7. We don't know who the Nicolaitans were. There are several theories, the most prominent being that the Nicolaitans were a sect teaching that a Christ-follower could commit immorality with immunity. What do we know for sure about the Nicolaitans based on the Scripture itself in Revelation 2:6 and 2:14–15?

> **2:6** "But you do have this going for you: You hate what the Nicolaitans practice—practices I also hate."

. . . .

> **2:14–15** "But I have a few things against you: You have some people there who follow the teaching of Balaam, who instructed Balak to put a stumbling block before the people of Israel so they would eat food sacrificed to idols and commit sexual immorality. In the same way, there are also some among you who follow the teaching of the Nicolaitans."

_____

_____

Apparently the false teachers in Ephesus were similar to Balaam. So consider the story about Balaam and Balak from the Old Testament.

After Israel came out of Egypt, we read in Numbers 22 about how the Israelites camped on the plains of Moab beside the Jordan River next to Jericho. The Moabites were terrified because of what Israel had already done to the Amorites. So Balak, king of the Moabites, sent messengers with money to Balaam, God's prophet, to summon him and ask him to curse Israel for them.

When Balaam heard their message, he told the messengers to stay and he would let them know what God told him. When God appeared to Balaam, he asked who the men were. Balaam told him, and God commanded, "You must not go with them; you must not curse the people, for they are blessed."

So Balaam sent the messengers home.

But Balak of Moab just sent a more numerous and distinguished group, who promised Balaam honor if he would curse Israel.

Balaam told them he didn't care about Balak's silver and gold. Yet he also invited the messengers to stay and told them he'd let them know what God had to say about it.

That night God appeared and told Balaam to go with them, and that he would tell him what to say. So Balaam went to Moab.

This angered God, and his angel stood in the road to oppose Balaam. When Balaam's donkey saw the angel with his sword drawn, he turned off the road and went into a field. So Balaam beat the donkey to make her go back to the road.

When the angel of the Lord stood in a walled path among the vineyards, the donkey saw the angel and pressed herself into the wall, crushing Balaam's foot. So he beat her again.

But the angel of the Lord stood in a narrow place, where there was no way to turn either to the right or to the left. When the donkey saw the angel of the Lord this time, she crouched under Balaam. That made Balaam angry, and he beat his donkey with a staff.

Then the Lord opened the donkey's mouth, and she spoke, asking Balaam, "What have I done to you that you have beaten me these three times?"

Balaaam said, "You have made me look stupid. If I had a sword, I'd kill you right now."

The donkey asked, "Have I ever attempted to treat you this way?"

"No."

The Lord opened Balaam's eyes, and he saw the angel of the Lord standing in the way with his sword drawn in his hand; so Balaam bowed his head and threw himself down with his face to the ground.

The angel asked Balaam why he was beating his donkey.

Balaam said, "I have sinned, for I did not know that you stood against me in the road. So now, if it is evil in your sight, I will go back home."

But the angel told him to go with the men and speak God's word. So Balaam went.

When Balak heard that Balaam was coming, he went out to meet him.

Balaam told him he must speak only the words God gave him. Then he accompanied Balak to a place where the king sacrificed bulls and sheep. And Balak sent some of the meat to Balaam and the princes. The next morning Balak took Balaam to a high place where he could see the whole nation.

Balaam told Balak, "Build me seven altars here, and prepare seven bulls and seven rams." So Balak did this, and both Balak and Balaam offered a bull and a ram on every altar.

Balaam said, "Station yourself by your burnt offering, and I will go off; perhaps the Lord will come to meet me, and whatever he reveals to me I will tell you." Then he went to a deserted height.

God met Balaam and put a message in his mouth to utter before Balak. In his message Balaam asked, "How can I curse one whom God has not cursed, or how can I denounce one whom the Lord has not denounced. . . . Let me die the death of the upright, and let the end of my life be like theirs."

This angered Balak, because it amounted to a curse on Moab.

Balaam explained that he had to say only God's words. So Balak asked Balaam to accompany him to a different place and curse Israel from there. And basically the same thing happened.

So Balak told Balaam, "Neither curse them at all nor bless them at all!"

But Balaam replied, "Didn't I tell you, 'All that the Lord speaks, I must do'?"

So Balak tried a third time from another place. Yet Balaam did not go as at the other times to seek for omens, but he set his face toward the wilderness. He uttered a blessing that included these words: "God brought them out of Egypt. They have, as it were, the strength of a young bull; they will devour hostile people and will break their bones and will pierce them through with arrows."

This made Balak furious, and he sent Balaam home. Balaam said, in essence, "I told you so," "and then he uttered a long curse on Moab and those who opposed Israel before going home."

8. What similarities do you see between Balaam and those who commit immorality and sacrifice to idols?

9. For which of the commendations mentioned in Revelation 2:2–3 would the Lord be able to commend you?

THURSDAY: THE BAD PROGNOSIS

1. Pray for insight; then read aloud our passage for the week:

> **Revelation 2:1** To the angel of the church in Ephesus, write the following:
>
> "This is the solemn pronouncement of the one who has a firm grasp on the seven stars in his right hand—the one who walks among the seven golden lampstands: **2:2** 'I know your works as well as your labor and steadfast endurance, and that you cannot tolerate evil. You have even put to the test those who refer to themselves as apostles (but are not), and have discovered that they are false. **2:3** I am also aware that you have persisted steadfastly, endured much for the sake of my name, and have not grown weary. **2:4** But I have this against you: You have departed from your first love! **2:5** Therefore, remember from what high state you have fallen and repent! Do the deeds you did at the first; if not, I will come to you and remove your lampstand from its place—that is, if you do not repent. **2:6** But you do have this going for you: You hate what the Nicolaitans practice—practices I also hate. **2:7** The one who has an ear had better hear what the Spirit says to the churches. To the one who conquers, I will permit him to eat from the tree of life that is in the paradise of God.'"

2. Circle all the references relating to work, deeds, practices, and labor. What is Christ's criticism of the Ephesian church (2:4)?

_____

_____

3. Are you in danger of leaving your first love now? What are some potential areas in your life that could cause you to leave your first love?

_____

_____

4. Reread Revelation 2:5:

> **2:5** "Therefore, remember from what high state you have fallen and repent! Do the deeds you did at the first; if not, I will come to you and remove your lampstand from its place—that is, if you do not repent."

What are the Lord's instructions to the church at Ephesus?

_____

_____

Why would it be important for the believers to remember from where they had fallen?

_____

_____

What is repentance and why is it necessary? Is repentance the same as saying you're sorry? What's the difference between remorse and repentance?

_____

_____

What is Jesus Christ implying when he says, "If not, I will remove your lampstand from its place"?

_____

_____

What deeds might fan the flames of your love for Christ and others?

_____

_____

5. Notice how the Lord includes affirmation along with warning. Why is this a wise approach when confronting others?

_____

_____

FRIDAY: WE SHALL OVERCOME SOME DAY

1. Pray for insight; then read Revelation 2:7 aloud.

> **2:7** "The one who has an ear had better hear what the Spirit says to the churches. To the one who conquers, I will permit him to eat from the tree of life that is in the paradise of God."

Scholars vary in their understanding about what Rev. 2:7 means. Some believe that _conquerors_ are a special class of believers; others think those who conquer are all believers.

2. How do the following Scriptures, possibly all penned by the same author, support the second view?

> **1 John 4:4** "You are from God, little children, and have conquered them, because the one who is in you is greater than the one who is in the world."

. . . .

> **1 John 5:4–5** "Because everyone who has been fathered by God conquers the world. This is the conquering power that has conquered the world: our faith. Now who is the person who has

conquered the world except the one who believes that Jesus is the Son of God?"

....

Revelation 21:5-7 "And the one seated on the throne said: 'Look! I am making all things new!' Then he said to me, 'Write it down, because these words are reliable and true.' He also said to me, 'It is done! I am the Alpha and the Omega, the beginning and the end. To the one who is thirsty I will give water free of charge from the spring of the water of life. The one who conquers will inherit these things, and I will be his God and he will be my son.'"

_____

_____

_____

3. What additional insight do we gain from the following passages about the "tree of life that is in the paradise of God"?

Genesis 2:8-9 "The Lord God planted an orchard in the east, in Eden; and there he placed the man he had formed. The Lord God made all kinds of trees grow from the soil, every tree that was pleasing to look at and good for food. (Now the tree of life and the tree of the knowledge of good and evil were in the middle of the orchard.)"

....

Genesis 3:22-24 "And the Lord God said, 'Now that the man has become like one of us, knowing good and evil, he must not be allowed to stretch out his hand and take also from the tree of life and eat, and live forever.' So the Lord God expelled him from the orchard in Eden to cultivate the ground from which he had been taken. When he drove the man out, he placed on the eastern side of the orchard in Eden angelic sentries who used the flame of a whirling sword to guard the way to the tree of life."

....

Luke 23:43 "And Jesus said to him, 'I tell you the truth, today you will be with me in paradise.'"

....

Revelation 22:1-2 "Then the angel showed me the river of the water of life—water as clear as crystal—pouring out from the throne of God and of the Lamb, flowing down the middle of the city's main street. On each side of the river is the tree of life producing twelve kinds of fruit, yielding its fruit every month of the year. Its leaves are for the healing of the nations."

_____

_____

4. What exactly is Jesus promising to those who emerge victorious when he says, "I will permit him to eat from the tree of life that is in the paradise of God"?

_____

_____

5. As you look back over the letter to the church in Ephesus, how would you summarize God's message to them?

_____

_____

6. How are you like the people in Ephesus in John's time? What are some lessons for life that you can draw from this passage that can be applied in your own life?

_____

_____

7. In this world we will have many adversaries. Yet Jesus promises us victory to overcome them all as we abide in him as overcomers. According to the following verses, who or what are our adversaries and what are the means for overcoming them?

> **John 16:33** "I have told you these things so that in me you may have peace. In the world you have trouble and suffering, but take courage—I have conquered the world."

. . . .

Galatians 5:16–17 "But I say, live by the Spirit and you will not carry out the desires of the flesh. For the flesh has desires that are opposed to the Spirit, and the Spirit has desires that are opposed to the flesh, for these are in opposition to each other, so that you cannot do what you want."

· ·

Ephesians 6:10–13 "Finally, be strengthened in the Lord and in the strength of his power. Clothe yourselves with the full armor of God so that you may be able to stand against the schemes of the devil. For our struggle is not against flesh and blood, but against the rulers, against the powers, against the world rulers of this darkness, against the spiritual forces of evil in the heavens. For this reason, take up the full armor of God so that you may be able to stand your ground on the evil day, and having done everything, to stand."

· ·

1 Peter 5:8–9 "Be sober and alert. Your enemy the devil, *like a roaring lion*, is on the prowl looking for someone to devour. Resist him, strong in your faith, because you know that your brothers and sisters throughout the world are enduring the same kinds of suffering."

8. Our service for Christ, our devotion to him, our commitment— they all come back to love. Think back to a time in your life when your love for God was strong, as evidenced by joyful service to him. Compare that time with where you are now. How are you doing? Of what do you need to repent?

9. Do you have undying love for Jesus, or is your love for him dying out? Pray that God would rekindle your love.

When my coauthor and I did the research for *Sexual Intimacy in Marriage* (Kregel), we heard from more than one husband who insisted he loved his wife but resented her objections to his going out with the guys several times a week. From their wives we'd hear, "He used to bring me flowers for no reason. Now all he brings me is dirty laundry."

Yet it wasn't just the husbands who'd lost their vigilance in fanning love flames. We also heard complaints like, "She used to tell me how much she appreciated me. Now she just points out what good husbands her *friends* have."

> "The cross is the blazing fire at which the flame of our love is kindled, but we have to get near enough to it for its sparks to fall on us." —John Stott

These stories remind me of a pathetic cartoon. In it a husband of many years opened his wife's car door, and his self-conscious partner told him, "Stop it! People will think we're not married!"

How can we gauge when love is alive? It shows itself in actions. Simply put, loving feelings can't help but show themselves in loving acts.

We've all seen it, haven't we? A friend falls in love, and for a while she won't even look at another guy. She's loyal. She swoons. She can't stop talking about her new man. But then her hot-blooded "love" cools off, and she gets lazy. Before long she's flirting with other guys. Sure, she insists, "I still love my man—but I can look, look, look as long as I don't touch."

We don't buy it, do we?

It's similar with our commitment to Christ. Often at the beginning of our faith walk, we act like a new bride, delirious with joy over our Groom. But then we find out how hard the Christian life can be. And we get jaded. God's people wound us. We grow weary. And then when we see other new believers' enthusiasm, we roll our eyes and try to warn them.

It's interesting that when Jesus rebuked the Ephesians for departing from their first love, he didn't say, "Return to your former affection." He told them to repent and return to their former works.

Now, some of us have a knee-jerk negative reaction to the word *works* when talking about the spiritual life, because too often people make good deeds a condition of salvation. But that's not what's happening here. Instead, Christ is indeed assessing the Ephesians' love by their actions, gauging their love by whether they do the works they did at first.

Maybe the Ephesians still hated the Nicolaitans' ways, but they were less vigilant about idolatry than in former days—sort of like Balaam. Balaam was mostly in the right camp in that he never actually cursed Israel. But why was he even talking to Israel's enemies? Why did he let them spend the night? If God had already told Balaam what to do, why did he invite the Moabites to camp out until he could assess whether he'd get another message? Balaam was way too friendly with those determined to bring down God's people.

We may worship different idols from those the Ephesians worshiped. The desire to hang out in the temples of Artemis and Athena don't make our lists of temptations. Yet we have our own idols—the stuff we love more than God—as evidenced by our actions. We mess around with sin, skirting too close to the edge of temptation. There's that guy at work we're too friendly with because he makes us feel good. Or maybe it's those hours we spend on the computer while we claim we can't fit Bible reading into our schedules. Or our prayerlessness because we depend on our own strength. Or the lyrics we recite and jam to while insisting we never were good at Scripture memorization. Or the holds we have on our material goods while others around the world ask, "Why isn't our rich family caring for us?" Or the grudges we nurse, the tongues we won't control, sloth, our endless pursuit of books or career goals or others' respect or movies or shopping or food or love or . . . chocolate.

What's the solution? Twice Jesus says, "Repent." And repenting goes far beyond mumbling "I'm sorry." It means by his power doing a 180. Making radical changes. Falling on our faces, agreeing with God, and getting serious about throwing out the enemy and slamming the door.

The one with such a magnificent obsession will eat of the tree of life in the paradise of God!

Pray: "Lord Jesus, give me a deeper repentance, a horror of sin, a dread of its approach. Help me chastely to flee it and jealously to resolve that my heart shall be Yours alone. Give me a deeper trust, that I may lose myself to find myself in You, the ground of my rest, the spring of my being. Give me a deeper knowledge of Yourself as savior, master, lord, and king. Give me deeper power in private prayer, more sweetness in Your Word, more steadfast grip on its truth. Give me deeper holiness in speech, thought, action, and let me not seek moral virtue apart from You. Plow deep in me, great Lord, heavenly husbandman, that my being may be a tilled field, the roots of grace spreading far and wide, until You alone art seen in me, Your beauty golden like summer harvest, Your fruitfulness as autumn plenty. I have no master but You, no law but Your will, no delight but Yourself, no wealth but that You give, no good but that You bless, no peace but that You bestow. I am nothing but that You make me. I have nothing but that I receive from You. I can be nothing but that grace adorns me. Quarry me deep, dear Lord, and then fill me to overflowing with living water."[6]

Memorize: "But I have this against you: You have departed from your first love! Therefore, remember from what high state you have fallen and repent! Do the deeds you did at the first; if not, I will come to you and remove your lampstand from its place—that is, if you do not repent" (Rev. 2:4–5).

---

[6] From *The Valley of Vision, http://www.oldlandmarks.com/puritan.htm#Devotion.*

WEEK 3 OF 8

Smyrna: The Suffering Church
Revelation 2:8–11

Scripture: "Remain faithful even to the point of death, and I will give you the crown that is life itself" (Rev. 2:10).

About thirty-five miles up the coast from Ephesus lies the seaport of Smyrna. Scripture provides no information about who planted the church there, but Paul may have traversed fertile fig, grape, and olive orchards between the cities with the gospel during his extended stay at Ephesus. Or perhaps a disciple from Ephesus carried the Good News to this neighboring town.

Today the site of ancient Smyrna, with its perfect climate, is the thriving Turkish city of Izmir, a variation on the ancient name. A beautiful port, the city is the largest in Asia Minor.

Izmir predates Christianity by more than a thousand years, and its ancient remains lie buried beneath bazaars, houses, and mosques. Still, in the middle of the hilly metropolis, Christian pilgrims find a large outdoor fenced square on top of which lie arches and pillars stacked as in a museum warehouse awaiting reconstruction.

What is today a mosque-filled, waterfront city was the site of immense suffering in New Testament times. Christians in ancient days were destitute because the business guilds disallowed Christ-followers. Imagine a layoff that never ends.

Most commentators, in fact, note that *Smyrna* is a Greek translation of the Old Testament Hebrew word *myrrh*. The process of making myrrh involves crushing a fragrant plant, and it has been said that the church at Smyrna, crushed by persecution, gave off a fragrant aroma to God.

Even today the persecution facing Christians is still the largest human rights violation in the world. According to the World Evangelical Alliance, over 200 million Christians in at least sixty countries are denied fundamental human rights solely because of their faith. And many of these, our brothers and sisters, endure valiantly.

International speaker Nik Ripken, who has researched the qualities of those who stand strong in the midst of such suffering, cites eleven characteristics of Christians who have remained faithful under intense persecution. Those who persevered

- know Jesus,
- know the power of prayer and fasting,
- know large portions of the Bible by memory,
- know large amounts of music by memory,
- know people are praying for them,
- know the local believing community is caring for their family,
- know that their suffering is for Jesus' sake,
- know their persecution is normal,
- have claimed their freedom,
- have lost their fear, and
- have a legacy of faith.

If you are not enduring persecution, why not? If you are, do you "pray for those who persecute you" (Matt. 5:44)? How are you caring for the families of those who are suffering? Are you praying that those persecuted would remain obedient in their time of trial, that they would be bold, and that God would use their suffering to draw others to himself? Those of us living in a time and place of relative ease must realize that our circumstances could change at any time. Are we, with God's help, seeking the above characteristics for ourselves and those we love?

1. Pray for insight; then read aloud Revelation 2:8–11.

> **2:8** To the angel of the church in Smyrna write the following:
>
> "This is the solemn pronouncement of the one who is the first and the last, the one who was dead, but came to life: **2:9** 'I know the distress you are suffering and your poverty (but you are rich). I also know the slander against you by those who call themselves Jews and really are not, but are a synagogue of Satan. **2:10** Do not be afraid of the things you are about to suffer. The devil is about to have some of you thrown into prison so you may be tested, and you will experience suffering for ten days. Remain faithful even to the point of death, and I will give you the crown that is life itself. **2:11** The one who has an ear had better hear what the Spirit says to the churches. The one who conquers will in no way be harmed by the second death.'"

2. In this message, what description of Jesus do you find?

_____

_____

What commendation for the church?

_____

_____

Any criticism? If so, what?

_____

_____

What consequence and exhortation?

_____

_____

What promise to the one who conquers?

_____

_____

Use your answers to fill in the chart included at the beginning of this study. Also locate Smyrna on the map.

3. How is Jesus described in verse 8, and which attribute(s) of God does this description emphasize? (Compare this with the description of Christ in Revelation 1:17–18.)

_____

_____

4. Why is the description of Christ for the church at Smyrna especially encouraging for this audience?

_____

_____

5. Compare the description given of Christ with the following Old Testament verses about God. How does the combination of verses affirm Christ's equality with God?

> **Isaiah 41:4** "Who acts and carries out decrees? Who summons the successive generations from the beginning? I, the Lord, am present at the very beginning, and at the very end—I am the one."
> . . . .
> **Isaiah 44:6** "This is what the Lord, Israel's king, says, their protector, the Lord who commands armies: 'I am the first and I am the last, there is no God but me.'"
> . . . .
> **Isaiah 48:12** "Listen to me, O Jacob, Israel, whom I summoned! I am the one; I am present at the very beginning and at the very end."

_____

_____

6. How do the following verses help us understand the meaning of Christ as he "who was dead, but came to life"?

> **Romans 6:8–9** "Now if we died with Christ, we believe that we will also live with him. We know that since Christ has been raised from the dead, he is never going to die again; death no longer has mastery over him."

· ·

> **Hebrews 2:14–15** "Therefore, since the children share in flesh and blood, he [Jesus] likewise shared in their humanity, so that through death he could destroy the one who holds the power of death (that is, the devil), and set free those who were held in slavery all their lives by their fear of death."

· ·

> **1 Peter 3:18** "Christ also suffered once for sins, *the just for the unjust*, to bring you to God, by being put to death in the flesh but by being made alive in the spirit."

---

7. Which of the above attributes most comfort you in the midst of trials? Why?

---

8. Have you experienced suffering during which you found it difficult to stand firm? If so, how did you handle the situation?

---

9. How could the following verses about Jesus Christ encourage you in the midst of tough times?

> **Hebrews 2:17–18** "Therefore he had to be made like his brothers and sisters in every respect, so that he could become a merciful and faithful high priest in things relating to God, to make atone-

ment for the sins of the people. For since he himself suffered when he was tempted, he is able to help those who are tempted."

. . . .

Hebrews 4:14–16 "Therefore since we have a great high priest who has passed through the heavens, Jesus the Son of God, let us hold fast to our confession. For we do not have a high priest incapable of sympathizing with our weaknesses, but one who has been tempted in every way just as we are, yet without sin. Therefore let us confidently approach the throne of grace to receive mercy and find grace whenever we need help."

. . . .

Hebrews 12:3 "Think of him who endured such opposition against himself by sinners, so that you may not grow weary in your souls and give up."

_____

_____

"When fear grips the human heart, and our very life is threatened, nothing can bring tranquility like faith in Him who is both the first and the last."—John Stott, *What Christ Thinks of the Church*

10. Offer praise to the Lord for who he is in light of the Scripture you read today. Write out your words of thanksgiving and consider putting them to music.

_____

_____

_____

TUESDAY: JESUS KNOWS

1. Pray for insight; then read aloud today's verse:

Revelation 2:9: "I know the distress you are suffering and your poverty (but you are rich). I also know the slander against you by those who call themselves Jews and really are not, but are a synagogue of Satan."

2. About what three things did Jesus say "I know" concerning the church at Smyrna?

_____

_____

3. How did Jesus use contrast to refer to how things appear and how they are in reality?

_____

_____

4. List as many different ways as you can in which a person can be rich.

_____

_____

I wrote the following one Friday after Thanksgiving. Can you relate? "I love hosting the dinner, having loved ones sleep on my couch, hanging out in front of the TV, working a puzzle, drinking wassail, and snacking on leftover turkey. I love the crowd of loved ones with the noise, the laughter, the teasing. I love it all because I believe the people in my life are one of my greatest sources of wealth. Congress can't destroy that. Nor can a lousy economy. I may not have a lot in the bank. Nevertheless, I am exceedingly, lavishly, decadently, abundantly rich, rich, rich, rich, rich. And I had nothing to do with it."

5. What kind of wealth does Jesus have in mind when he refers to the church at Smyrna as being rich in the midst of poverty?

_____

_____

6. Pray for insight; then read Ephesians 1:3–14. Underline the different benefits or riches a believer in Christ possesses.

> **1:3** "Blessed is the God and Father of our Lord Jesus Christ, who has blessed us with every spiritual blessing in the heavenly realms in Christ. **1:4** For he chose us in Christ before the foundation of the world that we may be holy and unblemished in his sight in love. **1:5** He did this by predestining us to adoption as his sons through Jesus Christ, according to the pleasure of his will—**1:6** to the praise of the glory of his grace that he has freely bestowed on us in his dearly loved Son. **1:7** In him we have redemption through his blood, the forgiveness of our trespasses, according to the riches of his grace **1:8** that he lavished on us in all wisdom and insight. **1:9** He did this when he revealed to us the secret of his will, according to his good pleasure that he set forth in Christ, **1:10** toward the administration of the fullness of the times, to head up all things in Christ—the things in heaven and the things on earth. **1:11** In Christ we too have been claimed as God's own possession, since we were predestined according to the one purpose of him who accomplishes all things according to the counsel of his will **1:12** so that we, who were the first to set our hope on Christ, would be to the praise of his glory. **1:13** And when you heard the word of truth (the gospel of your salvation)—when you believed in Christ—you were marked with the seal of the promised Holy Spirit, **1:14** who is the down payment of our inheritance, until the redemption of God's own possession, to the praise of his glory."

7. In what ways are you rich? Do you have the kind of wealth Jesus is talking about in Revelation 2:9?

---

8. How can you encourage someone being persecuted for his or her faith or suffering in attempts to love others with Jesus' love?

---

9. Why are those "who call themselves Jews and really are not" referred to as a "synagogue of Satan"? How does Romans 2:28–29 relate to this?

> **2:28** "For a person is not a Jew who is one outwardly, nor is circumcision something that is outward in the flesh, **2:29** but someone is a Jew who is one inwardly, and circumcision is of the heart by the Spirit and not by the written code. This person's praise is not from people but from God."

Note: The Greek word translated "slander" in Rev. 2:9 is *blasphemia*. The New American Standard Bible renders it as "blasphemy." Jesus' use of such a strong term was usually reserved for hostile words against God, indicating the slander's wickedness, intensity, and severity.[7]

_____

_____

10. Look at the conversation between Jesus and the Jews in John 8:31–37.

> **8:31** "Then Jesus said to those Judeans who had believed him, 'If you continue to follow my teaching, you are really my disciples **8:32** and you will know the truth, and the truth will set you free.'
>
> **8:33** "'We are descendants of Abraham,' they replied, 'and have never been anyone's slaves! How can you say, "You will become free"?'
>
> **8:34** "Jesus answered them, 'I tell you the solemn truth, everyone who practices sin is a slave of sin. **8:35** The slave does not remain in the family forever, but the son remains forever. **8:36** So if the son sets you free, you will be really free. **8:37** I know that you are Abraham's descendants. But you want to kill me, because my teaching makes no progress among you.'"

List reasons why those Jews were not considered true Jews in Jesus' eyes.

_____

_____

---

[7] John MacArthur, *New Testament Commentary on Revelation*, 71.

11. How does this compare with the strong terminology Jesus uses in Revelation 2:9?

_____

_____

12. Note that Jesus tells the church at Smyrna three things in today's text. He knows their distress, their poverty, and the slander they're enduring. Why do you think it comforted his listeners to hear "Jesus knows"?

_____

_____

13. What difficulty are you experiencing today as you seek to walk in faith? Jesus Christ knows! Write a prayer handing over the difficult situations on your heart to the one who knows and cares.

_____

_____

WEDNESDAY: TAKE THE LONG VIEW

1. Pray for insight; then read aloud Revelation 2:10:

> **2:10** "Do not be afraid of the things you are about to suffer. The devil is about to have some of you thrown into prison so you may be tested, and you will experience suffering for ten days. Remain faithful even to the point of death, and I will give you the crown that is life itself."

2. According to Revelation 2:10, what did the future hold for the church at Smyrna, and what would be the end result both physically and spiritually?

_____

_____

3. In the message to Smyrna what two commands and one promise do you find in Revelation 2:10?

_____

_____

4. As Revelation 2:10 indicates, Christians are not exempt from suffering. Scriptures that suggest some of the reasons God allows suffering in our lives include the following:

> **Romans 5:3–5** "Not only this, but we also rejoice in sufferings, knowing that suffering produces endurance, and endurance, character, and character, hope. And hope does not disappoint, because the love of God has been poured out in our hearts through the Holy Spirit who was given to us."

> **2 Corinthians 1:3–5** "Blessed is the God and Father of our Lord Jesus Christ, the Father of mercies and God of all comfort, who comforts us in all our troubles so that we may be able to comfort those experiencing any trouble with the comfort with which we ourselves are comforted by God. For just as the sufferings of Christ overflow toward us, so also our comfort through Christ overflows to you."

> **2 Corinthians 12:7–10** "Therefore, so that I would not become arrogant, a thorn in the flesh was given to me, a messenger of Satan to trouble me—so that I would not become arrogant. I asked the Lord three times about this, that it would depart from me. But he said to me, 'My grace is enough for you, for my power is made perfect in weakness.' So then, I will boast most gladly about my weaknesses, so that the power of Christ may reside in me. Therefore I am content with weaknesses, with insults, with troubles, with persecutions and difficulties for the sake of Christ, for whenever I am weak, then I am strong."

> **Hebrews 5:8** "Although he [Jesus] was a son, he learned obedience through the things he suffered."

> **Hebrews 12:4–11** "You have not yet resisted to the point of bloodshed in your struggle against sin. And have you forgotten the exhortation addressed to you as sons?

*'My son, do not scorn the Lord's discipline
or give up when he corrects you.
'For the Lord disciplines the one he loves and chastises every
son he accepts.'*

"Endure your suffering as discipline; God is treating you as sons. For what son is there that a father does not discipline? But if you do not experience discipline, something all sons have shared in, then you are illegitimate and are not sons. Besides, we have experienced discipline from our earthly fathers and we respected them; shall we not submit ourselves all the more to the Father of spirits and receive life? For they disciplined us for a little while as seemed good to them, but he does so for our benefit, that we may share his holiness. Now all discipline seems painful at the time, not joyful. But later it produces the fruit of peace and righteousness for those trained by it."

List some of the reasons for human suffering and the godly responses, according to these verses.

_____

_____

5. The believers in Smyrna were already in the midst of tribulation (v. 9) and Jesus had no rebuke or condemnation for them. What would be the result of further testing (v. 10)?

_____

_____

6. What do the following verses imply about persecution and the believer?

John 15:20 "Remember what I told you, 'A slave is not greater than his master.' If they persecuted me, they will also persecute you. If they obeyed my word, they will obey yours too."

. . . .

Philippians 1:29 "For it has been granted to you not only to believe in Christ but also to suffer for him, since you are encountering the same conflict that you saw me face and now hear that I am facing."

. . . .

2 Timothy 3:12 "Now in fact all who want to live godly lives in Christ Jesus will be persecuted."

7. As you consider a biblical view of human suffering, read Job 1:

Job 1

"There was a man in the land of Uz whose name was Job. And that man was pure and upright, one who feared God and turned away from evil. Seven sons and three daughters were born to him. His possessions included 7,000 sheep, 3,000 camels, 500 yoke of oxen, and 500 female donkeys; in addition he had a very great household. Thus he was the greatest of all the people in the east.

"Now his sons used to go and hold a feast in the house of each one in turn, and they would send and invite their three sisters to eat and to drink with them. When the days of their feasting were finished, Job would send for them and sanctify them; he would get up early in the morning and offer burnt offerings according to the number of them all. For Job thought, 'Perhaps my children have sinned and cursed God in their hearts.' This was Job's customary practice.

"Now the day came when the sons of God came to present themselves before the Lord—and Satan also arrived among them. The Lord said to Satan, 'Where have you come from?' And Satan answered the Lord, 'From roving about on the earth, and from walking back and forth across it.' So the Lord said to Satan, 'Have you considered my servant Job? There is no one like him on the earth, a pure and upright man, one who fears God and turns away from evil.'

"Then Satan answered the Lord, 'Is it for nothing that Job fears God? Have you not made a hedge around him and his household and all that he has on every side? You have blessed the work of his hands, and his livestock have increased in the land. But extend your hand and strike everything he has, and he will no doubt curse you to your face!'

"So the Lord said to Satan, 'All right then, everything he has is in your power. Only do not extend your hand against the man himself!' So Satan went out from the presence of the Lord.

"Now the day came when Job's sons and daughters were eating and drinking wine in their oldest brother's house, and a messenger came to Job, saying, 'The oxen were plowing and the donkeys were grazing beside them, and the Sabeans swooped down and carried them all away, and they killed the servants with the sword! And I—only I alone—escaped to tell you!'

"While this one was still speaking, another messenger arrived and said, 'The fire of God has fallen from heaven and has burned up the sheep and the servants—it has consumed them! And I—only I alone—escaped to tell you!'

"While this one was still speaking another messenger arrived and said, 'The Chaldeans formed three bands and made a raid on the camels and carried them all away, and they killed the servants with the sword! And I—only I alone—escaped to tell you!'

"While this one was still speaking another messenger arrived and said, 'Your sons and your daughters were eating and drinking wine in their oldest brother's house, and suddenly a great wind swept across the wilderness and struck the four corners of the house, and it fell on the young people, and they died! And I—only I alone—escaped to tell you!'

"Then Job got up and tore his robe. He shaved his head, and then he threw himself down with his face to the ground. He said, 'Naked I came from my mother's womb, and naked I will return there. The Lord gives, and the Lord takes away. May the name of the Lord be blessed!' In all this Job did not sin, nor did he charge God with moral impropriety."

If God is ultimately in control, why do you think he allows the accuser to bring tribulation into the lives of his faithful followers?

_____

_____

8. How do you respond to suffering and tribulation? What helps you endure?

_____

_____

9. What do the following verses teach us about persevering in the midst of tribulation and suffering?

2 Corinthians 4:7–10 "But we have this treasure in clay jars, so that the extraordinary power belongs to God and does not come from us. We are experiencing trouble on every side, but are

not crushed; we are perplexed, but not driven to despair; we are persecuted, but not abandoned; we are knocked down, but not destroyed, always carrying around in our body the death of Jesus, so that the life of Jesus may also be made visible in our body."

2 Corinthians 4:16–18 "Therefore we do not despair, but even if our physical body is wearing away, our inner person is being renewed day by day. For our momentary, light suffering is producing for us an eternal weight of glory far beyond all comparison because we are not looking at what can be seen but at what cannot be seen. For what can be seen is temporary, but what cannot be seen is eternal."

1 Peter 5:10 "And, after you have suffered for a little while, the God of all grace who called you to his eternal glory in Christ will himself restore, confirm, strengthen, and establish you."

"Suffering either gives me my self or it destroys my self. If you receive yourself in the fires of sorrow, God will make you nourishment for other people."—Oswald Chambers in *My Utmost for His Highest*

10. Often we hear Christians say, "God has a wonderful plan for your life." Yet in the Bible we read that the Christian should expect to suffer in a way that an unbeliever does not. How do you reconcile the idea of a wonderful plan with suffering "for a little while" (1 Peter 5:10)?

11. Consider the trials you are currently experiencing. In what ways are you allowing them, or could you allow them, to deepen your relationship with Christ instead of pushing you away from him?

12. List some of the many ways Jesus suffered while on earth.

_____

_____

13. Spend some time thanking Jesus for what he endured for you.

THURSDAY: CASTING CROWNS

1. Pray for an open heart to understand the Word; then read aloud Revelation 2:10, spoken to the church at Smyrna:

2:10 "Do not be afraid of the things you are about to suffer. The devil is about to have some of you thrown into prison so

you may be tested, and you will experience suffering for ten days. Remain faithful even to the point of death, and I will give you the crown that is life itself."

2. Review: what two instructions did Jesus give the church at Smyrna concerning the upcoming time of difficulty?

_____

_____

3. How is it possible to be fearless in the face of impending suffering?

_____

_____

4. Can you think of other times in Scripture where the Lord commands, "Fear not!" or "Do not be afraid"?

_____

_____

5. Is there anything in your life that is causing you to be fearful? Pray, giving it to the Lord, trusting his hand, and looking ahead to the blessings that await you eternally.

_____

_____

6. Most other major translations have, "I will give you the crown of life." The NET Bible used in this study has "the crown that is life itself." Why do you think the NET renders this differently? When Jesus refers to this crown, do you think he is referring to abundant and eternal life or to a literal crown for those who are faithful through tribulation on this earth—or to both?

_____

_____

7. What additional insight do the following verses give concerning the crown of life?

> **John 10:10** "The thief comes only to steal and kill and destroy; I have come so that they may have life, and may have it abundantly."

. . . .

> **1 Cor. 9:24–25** "Do you not know that all the runners in a stadium compete, but only one receives the prize? So run to win. Each competitor must exercise self-control in everything. They do it to receive a perishable crown, but we an imperishable one."

. . . .

> **James 1:12** "Happy is the one who endures testing, because when he has proven to be genuine, he will receive the crown of life that God promised to those who love him."

_____

_____

8. What does it mean to be "faithful even to the point of death"?

_____

_____

9. The crown of life is one of several "crowns" mentioned in Scripture:

> **1 Thess. 2:19** "For who is our hope or joy or crown to boast of before our Lord Jesus at his coming? Is it not of course you?"

. . . .

> **2 Tim. 4:6–8** "For I am already being poured out as an offering, and the time for me to depart is at hand. I have competed well; I have finished the race; I have kept the faith! Finally the crown of righteousness is reserved for me. The Lord, the righteous Judge, will award it to me in that day—and not to me only, but also to all who have set their affection on his appearing."

. . . .

> **1 Peter 5:4** "Then when the Chief Shepherd appears, you will receive the crown of glory that never fades away."

. . . .

Rev. 4:4 "In a circle around the throne were twenty-four other thrones, and seated on those thrones were twenty-four elders. They were dressed in white clothing and had golden crowns on their heads."

What other crowns besides the crown of life are mentioned, and to what do they refer?

_____

_____

10. Today a crown marks a member of a royal family or the winner of a beauty pageant. It's usually a jewel-studded head ornament made of gold or silver. But in first-century Asia, crowns usually were made of leaves such as laurel or oak and had a broader use. A crown was a badge of office or distinction. In Greece, victors received crowns as awards in both athletic and poetic competitions. In the Roman world, victors—both military and civilian—received crowns when they marched in triumph. Paul seems to have Greek and Roman images in mind when he talks about the crowns awaiting faithful believers in Christ. Consider the crowns Paul talks about and the reasons for which God will award crowns:

The imperishable crown (1 Cor. 9:24–27). Contrasted with a crown that wilts or passes away. Awarded to those who consistently bring the flesh under the Spirit's control, refusing to yield to its evil desires.

The crown of exultation (Phil. 4:1; 1 Thess. 2:19–20). Received by Christ's servants who faithfully share the good news of salvation.

The crown of righteousness (2 Tim. 4:7–8). Awarded to those righteous souls who live each day joyfully looking forward to Jesus' return.

The crown of life (James 1:12). Reserved for those who successfully endure temptation and suffering.

The crown of glory (1 Pet. 5:1–4). Given to the shepherd who cherishes, feeds, protects, and preserves God's people.

Summarize the kind of person these verses indicate God will reward with crowns. Do they describe you? Why or why not?

_____

_____

11. According to Revelation 4:9–11, what ultimately happens to the elders' crowns (and probably ours)?

> **Revelation 4:9–11** "And whenever the living creatures give glory, honor, and thanks to the one who sits on the throne, who lives forever and ever, the twenty-four elders throw themselves to the ground before the one who sits on the throne and worship the one who lives forever and ever, and they offer their crowns before his throne, saying:
>
>> 'You are worthy, our Lord and God,
>> to receive glory and honor and power,
>> since you created all things,
>> and because of your will they existed and were created!' "

_____

_____

12. Spend a few minutes thinking about your priorities, comparing them with what's important to God. Ask him to help you bring them in line with what matters most.

FRIDAY: CONQUER YOUR FEAR

1. Pray for insight; then read aloud Jesus' message to the church at Smyrna:

> **Revelation 2:8** To the angel of the church in Smyrna write the following:
>
> "This is the solemn pronouncement of the one who is the first and the last, the one who was dead, but came to life: **2:9** 'I know the distress you are suffering and your poverty (but you are rich). I also know the slander against you by those who call themselves Jews and really are not, but are a synagogue of Satan. **2:10** Do not be afraid of the things you are about to suffer. The devil is about to have some of you thrown into prison so you may be tested, and you will experience suffering for ten days. Remain faithful even to the point of death, and I will give you the crown that is life itself. **2:11** The one who has an ear had better hear what the Spirit says to the churches. The one who conquers will in no way be harmed by the second death.' "

2. What does Jesus promise to the one who conquers (2:11)?

_____

_____

3. According to Revelation 20:14–15 and 21:8, what is the second death and who will experience it?

> **Revelation 20:14–15** "Then Death and Hades were thrown into the lake of fire. This is the second death—the lake of fire. If anyone's name was not found written in the book of life, that person was thrown into the lake of fire."

> . . . .

> **Revelation 21:8** "But to the cowards, unbelievers, detestable persons, murderers, the sexually immoral, and those who practice magic spells, idol worshipers, and all those who lie, their place will be in the lake that burns with fire and sulfur. That is the second death."

_____

_____

4. What else do we learn about those over whom the second death has no power according to the following verse?

> **Revelation 20:6** "Blessed and holy is the one who takes part in the first resurrection. The second death has no power over them, but they will be priests of God and of Christ, and they will reign with him for a thousand years."

_____

_____

5. Why would the promise about overcoming the second death be especially encouraging for the church at Smyrna?

_____

_____

6. Consider Jesus' words in Luke 12:4–7. What truths expressed in Jesus' words would encourage someone who is about to suffer for his faith?

> **12:4–7** "I tell you, my friends, do not be afraid of those who kill the body, and after that have nothing more they can do. But I will warn you whom you should fear: Fear the one who, after the killing, has authority to throw you into hell. Yes, I tell you, fear him! Aren't five sparrows sold for two pennies? Yet not one of them is forgotten before God. In fact, even the hairs on your head are all numbered. Do not be afraid; you are more valuable than many sparrows."

_____

_____

7. Do you fear God more than people? Are you a God pleaser more than a people pleaser? If so, how is that evident in your life?

_____

_____

8. What does 1 Peter 5:6–11 teach us about our adversary in the spiritual realm?

> **5:6–11** "And God will exalt you in due time, if you humble yourselves under his mighty hand by casting all your cares on him because he cares for you. Be sober and alert. Your enemy the devil, _like a roaring lion_, is on the prowl looking for someone to devour. Resist him, strong in your faith, because you know that your brothers and sisters throughout the world are enduring the same kinds of suffering. And, after you have suffered for a little while, the God of all grace who called you to his eternal glory in Christ will himself restore, confirm, strengthen, and establish you. To him belongs the power forever. Amen."

_____

_____

9. Compare the 1 Peter passage with the letter to the church at Smyrna (Rev. 2:8–11). What similarities do you find?

_____

_____

10. What else do you find about the adversary and those who overcome him from Revelation 12:9–11?

> **12:9–11** "So that huge dragon—the ancient serpent, the one called the devil and Satan, who deceives the whole world—was thrown down to the earth, and his angels along with him. Then I heard a loud voice in heaven saying,
>
> 'The salvation and the power
> and the kingdom of our God,
> and the ruling authority of his Christ, have now come,
> because the accuser of our brothers and sisters,
> the one who accuses them day and night before our God,
> has been thrown down.
> But they overcame him
> by the blood of the Lamb
> and by the word of their testimony,
> and they did not love their lives so much that they were
> afraid to die.'"

_____

_____

_____

11. The accuser planned to cast some of the Smyrna church into prison. How is he described in Revelation 2:8–11, and how does he work against believers?

> The Greek word _diabolos_ can be translated "devil" or "one who slanders." The word _satan_ means "accuser" or "adversary." These are technically descriptions, not proper names.

_____

_____

12. According to the various verses you've read today, how do believers overcome the accuser?

_____

_____

13. For the person who does not have the Holy Spirit's help to conquer, such words sound a call to repent and trust in Christ alone for salvation. The words in Revelation were intended to encourage, not frighten, believers. Yet sometimes when a believer reads such predictions, he or she trembles with doubt, afraid of facing the second death. Often someone will talk away such fear by thinking, I was saved on such-and-such a date. But a more biblical response would be to take inventory of character: Do I demonstrate I have trusted Christ? Does my life give evidence of the Holy Spirit's work? Am I willing to suffer? Am I overcoming temptation? Am I serving the accuser or the One who will reign forever? Our assurance comes from seeing God's work in our lives.

Are you secure concerning your eternal destiny? Why or why not?

_____

_____

"Our congregation may not be a Smyrna church just now. But we do experience our own pressures, suffering, and afflictions. And whenever we do, the vision of Jesus standing among us in all His glory, and the words of promise He speaks, will sustain and guide us."—Dr. Larry Richards, _The Teacher's Commentary_

14. Examine your heart. Ask God what he wants to teach you from this letter to the church at Smyrna. What is one area in your life needing your attention?

_____

_____

15. Go to a site such as www.persecution.com or the Web site for Voice of the Martyrs. Read the story of a modern-day martyr and pray for that person's church and family. Then find out what else you can do to help.

Before AD 100, John the Elder ordained a bishop in Smyrna named Polycarp.[8] Fifty-five years later, after a long life of serving Christ's church, the aged Polycarp was led to the stadium and brought before the proconsul.

The proconsul said, "Have respect to your old age. . . . Swear by the fortune of Cæsar; repent, and say, 'Away with the Atheists.'" (He used the word *atheist* because the early Christians were considered godless for refusing to worship the Roman pantheon.) The proconsul continued, "Swear, and I will set you at liberty. Reproach Christ."

To this Polycarp declared, "Eighty and six years have I served Him, and He never did me any harm: how then can I blaspheme my King and my Savior?"[9]

At that time, a segment of Jews in Smyrna so loathed Christianity that they broke Sabbath to gather wood for Polycarp's burning. And like Polycarp's younger contemporary, Ignatius of Antioch, Polycarp laid down his life for his Lord.

In a day in which faithlessness reigns, Polycarp leaves us this great testimony of faithfulness unto death. But he leaves us something else. A copy of one of his second-century letters, an epistle to the church at Philippi, serves to validate the authenticity of several biblical books. In the letter's brief two hundred lines, Polycarp cites phrases from twelve New Testament writings, including Matthew, 1 Peter, 1 John, and nine of Paul's epistles. Three of these Pauline epistles (1 and 2 Timothy and Ephesians) have early dates that have been disputed in recent years. Yet the fact that Polycarp thought and breathed and spoke and wrote Scripture, even lacing his own letter with constant Scripture references, helps silence critics who want to undermine the ancient manuscripts of the faith.

[8] Iren., iii.3, 4.
[9] From www.newadvent.org/fathers/0102.htm

The church at Smyrna was one of only two of the seven churches to whom Christ had no words of rebuke. This suffering body of believers received only his praise. Jesus encouraged the believers in Smyrna to stand strong despite intense tribulation, even if that meant facing physical death—which it did. Some things are more important than life itself. And the one who stands firm for the faith has a promise of ultimate reward that lies beyond this earth.

Omar Khalafe had such firmness. Instrumental in the spread of the gospel in Somalia, he had baptized many converts. But in September of 2009, Islamic militants controlling a security checkpoint killed him when they found him carrying twenty-five Somali Bibles. After shooting him, the militants placed the Bibles on top of Omar's body as a warning to others. Tragic! Yet in the grand scheme of things, who is worse off—Omar or those who killed only his body?

Are you enduring suffering? If so, is it for the right reason? Are you supporting those suffering for Christ? What are you willing to endure for the faith? Maybe God is not asking you to die. But he does require you to lay down your life—your *whole* life. Ask God to strengthen your faith so that you can endure victoriously. Stand strong. Are you building your life around what's worth dying for?

Pray: Lord Jesus Christ, you are the way. Thank you for providing the way to escape the second death. Your death on the cross means I will never have to experience the penalty for my own sin. Thank you for rescuing me in your love. Thank you for this amazing intersection of the Father's righteous justice and compassionate love. Grant me, through your Spirit, that I might never fear humans more than I revere Father, Son, and Holy Spirit. Grant me the grace to daily take up my cross and follow you, no matter what the cost. You are worthy! And because of your finished work, I have access to the Father to pray in your name. Amen.

Memorize: "Remain faithful even to the point of death, and I will give you the crown that is life itself" (Rev. 2:10).

WEEK 4 OF 8

Pergamum: The Compromising Church
Revelation 2:12–17

SUNDAY: WISDOM, LOVE, VIRGINITY—AND SATAN?

Scripture: "I know where you live—where Satan's throne is. Yet you continue to cling to my name and you have not denied your faith in me, even in the days of Antipas, my faithful witness, who was killed in your city where Satan lives" (Rev. 2:13).

When I was in elementary school, the extent of my education about Greek gods and goddesses was this little rhyme I learned from a family member: "Aphrodite's the one without a nightie." Helpful, huh?

Then in my teens someone taught me that all Greek goddesses were into sex, rendering the term *sex goddess* redundant. As it turns out, this isn't true.

During four years at a Christian college, I never heard mention of the Greek gods other than references that occur in the Book of Acts, such as Mars of Mars Hill, Zeus, and Hermes.

These combined experiences leave me with the conclusion that most Christians know little about the Greek pantheon. And should we care?

Actually, as it turns out, we should. When I visited Corinth for the first time, the tour guide told our group that Western visitors seem generally uninterested in ancient gods and goddesses. Yet knowing what member of the pantheon a city worshiped is essential to understanding that city's mentality. The more I thought about that, the more sense it made.

Consider Corinth itself. Aphrodite's temple towered atop the *Acrocorinth*, the mountain adjacent to the city. Pausanias, the ancient Greek historian wrote, "On the summit of the *Acrocorinthus* is a temple of Aphrodite. The images are Aphrodite armed, Helius, and Eros with a bow."[10]

Aphrodite was the goddess of love, and I don't mean the *agape* version. If you go to Corinth today and stand on the street where Paul probably sold tents, you can't miss seeing where her temple used to be. Everywhere you walk, you notice the Acrocorinth jutting up to the skies.

Now, if you know anything about the church in ancient Corinth, you know the people there struggled with all manner of sexual issues. And I wonder . . . might the presence of Aphrodite's cult there explain why? Could that be why Paul told the Corinthians that it was good for a man not to touch a woman (1 Cor. 7:1)? Is that why he affirmed the decision of singles to live a lifetime of sexual abstinence rather than marrying? Could this explain why a city that advertised itself as the love capital would receive Paul's beautiful treatise on true love— known to us as the love chapter (see 1 Cor. 13)?

<hr />

[10] Pausanias, *Geography*, 2.5.1. . .

Knowing a city's gods and goddesses can help us understand more about the messages sent to them by the apostles.

Think about Athens. Its goddess, Athena, was the goddess of wisdom, so citizens of Athens wanted their city to reflect culture, religion, and philosophy. And sure enough, in Acts 17 we read about Stoic and Epicurean philosophers conversing there. When Paul glanced around Athens, he saw a lot of altars to false gods. It was a city full of empty religion. Yet rather than dissing it, he zeroed in on the "altar to an unknown God." He went on to explain that the God unknown to them was the one true God, the one made without hands.

Then there's the virgin Artemis, protector of Ephesus. Artemis, contrary to what I heard about goddesses, didn't "do" sex. Artemis was the goddess of midwifery and also goddess of the hunt. Normally we think of women as gatherers and men as hunters, but not when it comes to Artemis. In Ephesus we find stonework with the Amazon story, and guides tell visitors that the city was founded by an Amazon queen. It's no coincidence then that 1 Timothy, written to Paul's protégé in Ephesus, includes extensive instructions about widows, challenges to women teaching false doctrines, and instruction for young widows to marry and have children.

All this helps us when we come to Pergamum. To get to ancient Pergamum, you pass through the modern city of Bergama at the base of another steep hill. You'll wind up, up, up a narrow road until you reach the old city's heights. After stepping up to the railing, you can look down on the panorama, and under a small grove of trees you'll see the scattered remains of the temple of Zeus. Zeus was the god of the sky and thunder. The father of Artemis, Apollo, Athena (and numerous others), Zeus was considered the ruler of Olympus and the big daddy of all the gods.

Might the presence of Zeus's temple be what Jesus was referring to when he spoke of Pergamum's "throne of Satan"? In John's day, at the top of Pergamum's eight-hundred-foot-high conical hill, Zeus's four-story structure projected on an edge of rock that may have looked like a huge seat. Christians probably shuddered as they saw smoke rising from animal sacrifices offered at "Satan's throne."

The backgrounds about these cities' gods and goddesses and the difficulties believers in each location faced can provide insight for us into living for Christ in contemporary cities full of worldly wisdom, immorality, and a low view of family. To the believers in Pergamum, Jesus said, "I know where you live—where Satan's throne is—yet you continue to cling to my name and you have not denied your faith in me, even in the days of Antipas, my faithful witness." Jesus knew.

What are the gods of your city? Greed? Immorality? Pride and image control? Materialism? Beauty and youth? Do you struggle to live by faith in a place where the evil one has a stronghold? Jesus knows. And by his grace he wants you to hold fast and be a witness. Will you rise to the challenge?

MONDAY: JESUS THE JUDGE

We don't know who planted the church at Pergamum. According to Acts 16:7–8, Paul passed through the region of Mysia, where Pergamum was located, on his second missionary journey. Yet we have no record that Paul preached the gospel or even visited the city. Most likely, Paul or a disciple from Ephesus founded this church during or after Paul's ministry at Ephesus (Acts 19:10) about the time the gospel was preached throughout Asia.[11]

1. Read Revelation 2:12–17. Today we will focus on verse 12, but read the entire letter to get an overview of the message to the church at Pergamum.

> **2:12** To the angel of the church in Pergamum write the following:
>
> "This is the solemn pronouncement of the one who has the sharp double-edged sword: **2:13** 'I know where you live—where Satan's throne is. Yet you continue to cling to my name and you have not denied your faith in me, even in the days of Antipas, my faithful witness, who was killed in your city where Satan lives. **2:14** But I have a few things against you: You have some people there who follow the teaching of Balaam, who instructed Balak to put a stumbling block before the people of Israel so they would eat food sacrificed to idols and commit sexual immorality. **2:15** In the same way, there are also some among you who follow the teaching of the Nicolaitans. **2:16** Therefore, repent! If not, I will come against you quickly and make war against those people with the sword of my mouth. **2:17** The one who has an ear had better hear what the Spirit says to the churches. To the one who conquers, I will give him some of the hidden manna, and I will give him a white stone, and on

[11] MacArthur, *84.*

that stone will be written a new name that no one can understand except the one who receives it.'"

2 . In this message, what description of Jesus do you find?

_____

_____

What commendation for the church?

_____

_____

What criticism?

_____

_____

What consequence and exhortation?

_____

_____

What promise to the one who conquers?

_____

_____

Use your answers to fill in the chart included at the beginning of this study. Also locate Pergamum on the map.

3. Jesus describes himself as the "one who has the sharp double-edged sword." What two things does *sword* symbolize in the following verses?

Ephesians 6:17 "And take *the helmet of salvation* and the sword of the Spirit, which is the word of God."

Revelation 2:16 "Therefore, repent! If not, I will come against you quickly and make war against those people with the sword of my mouth."

4. How does Revelation 19:11–16 support this symbolism and the purpose of this sword?

19:11 "Then I saw heaven opened and here came a white horse! The one riding it was called 'Faithful' and 'True,' and with justice he judges and goes to war. **19:12** His eyes are like a fiery flame and there are many diadem crowns on his head. He has a name written that no one knows except himself. **19:13** He is dressed in clothing dipped in blood, and he is called the Word of God. **19:14** The armies that are in heaven, dressed in white, clean, fine linen, were following him on white horses. **19:15** From his mouth extends a sharp sword, so that with it he can strike the nations. He will rule them with an iron rod, and he stomps the winepress of the furious wrath of God, the All-Powerful. **19:16** He has a name written on his clothing and on his thigh: 'King of kings and Lord of lords.'"

> *If it seems unusual to you that the sword of the Word is sometimes said to come from Jesus' mouth rather than from His book, remember that the printing press didn't come along until 1440. Prior to that, most people thought of the Word as spoken, not written.*

• *Make war . . . with the sword of my mouth* (2:16). Perhaps the sword has symbolic meaning—representing, for example, the Word of God. Yet here's another possibility. Perhaps it also refers to a more literal sword, a weapon. Consider that the Pergamon Altar was a monumental structure originally built in the second-century BC on one of the many terraces on Pergamum's acropolis. Today this altar has been reassembled in Berlin. The base, decorated with a frieze in high relief, depicts the battle between the Giants and the Olympian gods (see p. 90). Visitors to Pergamum at the time of the altar's construction would have first seen the frieze on the eastern face on which the artist had depicted the Greek gods Hera, Heracles, Zeus, Athena, and Ares engaged in battle, carrying various weapons. With this in mind, consider the image of Christ in Revelation 2:16, which says, "Therefore, repent! If not, I will come against you quickly and make war against those people with the sword of my mouth." Many pagans believed the gods would war against the Christians for being "atheists"—so called because they did not believe in the Greek pantheon. Perhaps Jesus is saying they have it backwards. Who is the *real* God here?

5. Why is this description of Christ especially appropriate for the church at Pergamum?

_____

_____

6. Describe the Word of God in Hebrews 4:12–13.

> **4:12** "For the word of God is living and active and sharper than any double-edged sword, piercing even to the point of dividing soul from spirit, and joints from marrow; it is able to judge the desires and thoughts of the heart. **4:13** And no creature is hidden from God, but everything is naked and exposed to the eyes of him to whom we must render an account."

_____

_____

7. How does the Word judge the intentions and thoughts of the heart?

_____

_____

_____

8. Can you give an example of a time when God's Word convicted your heart of an attitude or action?

_____

_____

9. What do you learn about Jesus as judge in these verses?

1 Corinthians 4:5 "So then, do not judge anything before the time. Wait until the Lord comes. He will bring to light the hidden things of darkness and reveal the motives of hearts. Then each will receive recognition from God."

· ·

James 4:12 "But there is only one who is lawgiver and judge— the one who is able to save and destroy. On the other hand, who are you to judge your neighbor?"

· ·

James 5:9 "Do not grumble against one another, brothers and sisters, so that you may not be judged. See, the judge stands before the gates!"

_____

_____

10. How should the truth in these verses affect your actions? Give an example.

_____

_____

11. The Scriptures indicate that sometimes love requires us to confront others and hold them accountable for their actions. Yet these verses indicate it's the job of Jesus Christ, who knows each heart, and not our place to judge. What's the difference?

_____

_____

12. Are you presently judging someone else? If so, confess it.

13. Take a few moments to meditate on the following verses. Allow the Word to penetrate your heart, reveal wrong motives, and lead you in the right way.

> **Psalm 139:23** Examine me, and probe my thoughts!
> Test me, and know my concerns!
> **139:24** See if there is any idolatrous tendency in me,
> and lead me in the reliable ancient path!

Jot down any thoughts the Spirit brings to mind.

_____

_____

TUESDAY: STAND FIRM

1. Pray for the Spirit to grant you insight; then read Revelation 2:12–13. For what did Jesus commend this church?

> **2:12** To the angel of the church in Pergamum write the following: "This is the solemn pronouncement of the one who has the sharp double-edged sword: **2:13** ' I know where you live—where Satan's throne is. Yet you continue to cling to my name and you have not denied your faith in me, even in the days of Antipas, my faithful witness, who was killed in your city where Satan lives.'"

_____

_____

_____

2. List the two evidences of the Pergamum church's faithfulness according to this verse.

_____

_____

- *Antipas, my faithful witness, who was killed in your city* (2:13). This reference to Antipas is the only one found in the Bible. All we know for certain about Antipas is that he was a contemporary of the apostle John who was martyred in Pergamum and known to John's audience, and who exhibited a faithfulness that brought him mention in the pages of Scripture. According to a tenth-century Christian tradition, John ordained Antipas as bishop of Pergamum during the reign of Domitian. In this story, Antipas was martyred around 92 AD by burning in a brazen, bull-shaped altar used for casting out demons worshipped by the local population. The word *antipas* means "against all," and the legend might have emerged around this meaning. Other ancient traditions suggest that the name Antipas is symbolic and actually refers either to Timothy or Athanasius of Alexandria.

> Prefer to learn history from a novel? *The Lost Letters of Pergamum* by Bruce W. Longenecker and Ben Witherington is a work of biblical fiction that introduces readers to the style of New Testament writings. It also presents the social and political world of Jesus and his first followers, as well as early Christian gatherings. Told by correspondence through ancient letters, the gripping plot mixes fact and fiction to paint an interesting and informative picture of the New Testament world and early Christianity.

3. The Christians in Pergamum remained faithful even when a brother endured martyrdom for his faith. Imagine what it would be like to watch people you love killed for their faith. Describe how you think that would affect you.

_____

_____

4. According to Ephesians 6:10–18, what provision has been made for believers in Christ to stand firm for him? List the specific instructions.

> **6:10** "Finally, be strengthened in the Lord and in the strength of his power. **6:11** Clothe yourselves with the full armor of God so that you may be able to stand against the schemes of the devil. **6:12** For our struggle is not against flesh and blood, but against the rulers, against the powers, against the world rulers of this darkness, against the spiritual forces of evil in the heavens. **6:13** For

this reason, take up the full armor of God so that you may be able to stand your ground on the evil day, and having done everything, to stand. **6:14** Stand firm therefore, by fastening the belt of truth around your waist, by putting on the breastplate of righteousness, **6:15** by fitting your feet with the preparation that comes from the good news of peace, **6:16** and in all of this, by taking up the shield of faith with which you can extinguish all the flaming arrows of the evil one. **6:17** And take *the helmet of salvation* and the sword of the Spirit, which is the word of God. **6:18** With every prayer and petition, pray at all times in the Spirit, and to this end be alert, with all perseverance and requests for all the saints."

_____

_____

5. Are you taking full advantage of the resources God has given you to help you stand firm? In which of the areas of Ephesians 6 are you strongest? Weakest?

_____

_____

6. Pergamum was a place where Satan ruled. What evidences of Satan's rule do you see in your home, community, city, and world?

_____

_____

7. What are some examples of ways in which believers may subtly deny Christ?

_____

_____

8. In Daniel 3, we read about how King Nebuchadnezzar made an image of gold before which the people were to fall down and worship. The penalty for refusing to worship? Being cast into a furnace of

Visitors can view reconstructed monumental buildings from Pergamum in Berlin, Germany's *Pergamonmuseum*. Situated on the Museum Island, The Pergamon Museum (also called The Pergamon) houses structures, such as the Pergamon Altar, consisting of parts transported from the original excavation sites. Not going to Germany anytime soon? You can find many photos from the museum on the Internet.

blazing fire. As you read Daniel 3:12–30, what observations do you make about Shadrach, Meshach, and Abednego and their steadfast faith in the midst of tribulation?

3:12 "'But there are Jewish men whom you appointed over the administration of the province of Babylon—Shadrach, Meshach, and Abednego—and these men have not shown proper respect to you, O king. They don't serve your gods and they don't pay homage to the golden statue that you have erected.'

3:13 "Then Nebuchadnezzar in a fit of rage demanded that they bring Shadrach, Meshach, and Abednego before him. So they brought them before the king. **3:14** Nebuchadnezzar said to them, 'Is it true, Shadrach, Meshach, and Abednego, that you don't serve my gods and that you don't pay homage to the golden statue that I erected? **3:15** Now if you are ready, when you hear the sound of the horn, flute, zither, trigon, harp, pipes, and all kinds of music, you must bow down and pay homage to the statue that I had made. If you don't pay homage to it, you will immediately be thrown into the midst of the furnace of blazing fire. Now, who is that god who can rescue you from my power?' **3:16** Shadrach, Meshach, and Abednego replied to King Nebuchadnezzar, 'We do not need to give you a reply concerning this. **3:17** If our God whom we are serving exists, he is able to rescue us from the furnace of blazing fire, and he will rescue us, O king, from your power as well. **3:18** But if not, let it be known to you, O king, that we don't serve your gods, and we will not pay homage to the golden statue that you have erected.'

3:19 "Then Nebuchadnezzar was filled with rage, and his disposition changed toward Shadrach, Meshach, and Abednego. He gave orders to heat the furnace seven times hotter than it was normally heated. **3:20** He ordered strong soldiers in his army to tie up Shadrach, Meshach, and Abednego and to throw them into the furnace of blazing fire. **3:21** So those men were tied up while still wearing their cloaks, trousers, turbans, and other clothes, and were thrown into the furnace of blazing fire. **3:22** But since the king's command was so urgent, and the furnace was so excessively hot, the men who escorted Shadrach, Meshach, and Abednego were killed by the leaping flames. **3:23** But those three men, Shadrach, Meshach, and Abednego, fell into the furnace of blazing fire while still securely bound.

3:24 "Then King Nebuchadnezzar was startled and quickly got up. He said to his ministers, 'Wasn't it three men that we tied up and threw into the fire?' They replied to the king, 'For sure, O king.' **3:25** He answered, 'But I see four men, untied and walking around in the midst of the fire! No harm has come to them! And the appearance of the fourth is like that of a god!' **3:26** Then Nebuchadnezzar approached the door of the furnace of blazing fire. He called out, 'Shadrach, Meshach, and Abednego, servants of the most high God, come out! Come here!'

"Then Shadrach, Meshach, and Abednego emerged from the fire. **3:27** Once the satraps, prefects, governors, and ministers of the king had gathered around, they saw that those men were physically unharmed by the fire. The hair of their heads was not singed, nor were their trousers damaged. Not even the smell of fire was to be found on them!

3:28 "Nebuchadnezzar exclaimed, 'Praised be the God of Shadrach, Meshach, and Abednego, who has sent forth his angel and has rescued his servants who trusted in him, ignoring the edict of the king and giving up their bodies rather than serve or pay homage to any god other than their God! **3:29** I hereby decree that any people, nation, or language group that blasphemes the god of Shadrach, Meshach, or Abednego will be dismembered and his home reduced to rubble! For there exists no other god who can deliver in this way.' **3:30** Then Nebuchadnezzar promoted Shadrach, Meshach, and Abednego in the province of Babylon."

_____

_____

9. How did the steadfast faith of Shadrach, Meshach, and Abednego affect Nebuchadnezzar?

_____

_____

10. Jesus Christ prohibits us from loving our lives more than we love him. What cost are you currently paying for the sake of Christ? What cost are you willing to pay?

_____

_____

11. We see from the example of Antipas and the church in Pergamum that it's possible to hold to the truth in the midst of severe attack. How are you doing in the area of steadfastness and faithful witness for Christ?

_____

_____

12. Meditate on 1 Corinthians 15:58:

> **15:58** "So then, dear brothers and sisters, be firm. Do not be moved! Always be outstanding in the work of the Lord, knowing that your labor is not in vain in the Lord."

What do you think this verse means?

_____

_____

13. Pray for yourself and your fellow believers that you will "be firm." Pray also for the persecuted church around the world that God would grant them the grace to remain faithful, and that he would spread the gospel through their witness. To help you stay focused, you can write out your prayer here:

_____

_____

14. Pass it on. Might another believer benefit from knowing you appreciate that he or she is standing fast? Whom can you call or send a note of encouragement?

_____

WEDNESDAY: DEALING WITH SIN AS A GROUP

1. Pray for insight and openness to the Spirit's leading; then read aloud Revelation 2:12–15.

> **2:12** To the angel of the church in Pergamum write the following:
>
> "This is the solemn pronouncement of the one who has the sharp double-edged sword: **2:13** "I know where you live—where Satan's throne is. Yet you continue to cling to my name and you have not denied your faith in me, even in the days of Antipas, my faithful witness, who was killed in your city where Satan lives. **2:14** But I have a few things against you: You have some people there who follow the teaching of Balaam, who instructed Balak to put a stumbling block before the people of Israel so they would eat food sacrificed to idols and commit sexual immorality. **2:15** In the same way, there are also some among you who follow the teaching of the Nicolaitans.'"

2. What was Jesus' concern or criticism about the church at Pergamum?

_____

_____

3. How do Jesus' concerns about the church at Pergamum differ from his concerns for Ephesus in Revelation 2:4–7?

> **Rev. 2:4** "But I have this against you: You have departed from your first love! **2:5** Therefore, remember from what high state you have fallen and repent! Do the deeds you did at the first; if not, I will come to you and remove your lampstand from its place—that is, if you do not repent. **2:6** But you do have this going for you: You hate what the Nicolaitans practice—practices I also hate. **2:7** The one who has an ear had better hear what the Spirit says to the churches. To the one who conquers, I will permit him to eat from the tree of life that is in the paradise of God."

_____

_____

You will recall that in week 2 we considered the story of Balaam. We find Balaam's story in Numbers 22–25. Fearful of the Israelites because of what they had done to the Amorites, Balak, king of Moab, hired the prophet Balaam to curse Israel. The story continues beyond what we read. After trying unsuccessfully three times to curse Israel, Balaam came up with another plan. He advised having Moabite women seduce Israelite men into intermarriage in order to corrupt them. This resulted in Israel participating in both sexual immorality and idol-worship feasts.

4. What do we learn about Balaam and his teaching from the following verses?

> **2 Peter 2:15–16** "By forsaking the right path they have gone astray, because they followed the way of Balaam son of Bosor, who loved the wages of unrighteousness, **2:16** yet was rebuked for his own transgression (a dumb donkey, speaking with a human voice, restrained the prophet's madness)."

> **Revelation 2:14** "But I have a few things against you: You have some people there who follow the teaching of Balaam, who instructed Balak to put a stumbling block before the people of Israel so they would eat food sacrificed to idols and commit sexual immorality."

5. In 1 Corinthians 5:1–8, we read about a situation in the first-century Corinthian church. How was the situation similar to what was happening in the church at Pergamum?

> **5:1** "It is actually reported that sexual immorality exists among you, the kind of immorality that is not permitted even among the Gentiles, so that someone is cohabiting with his father's wife. **5:2** And you are proud! Shouldn't you have been deeply sorrowful instead and removed the one who did this from among you? **5:3** For even though I am absent physically, I am present in spirit. And I have already judged the one who did this, just as though I were present. **5:4** When you gather together in the name of our Lord Jesus, and I am with you in spirit, along with the power of our Lord Jesus, **5:5** turn this man over to Satan for the destruction of the flesh, so that his spirit may be saved in the day of the Lord.
>
> **5:6** Your boasting is not good. Don't you know that a little yeast affects the whole batch of dough? **5:7** Clean out the old yeast so that you may be a new batch of dough—you are, in fact, without yeast. For Christ, our Passover lamb, has been sacrificed. **5:8** So then, let us celebrate the festival, not with the old yeast, the yeast of vice and evil, but with the bread without yeast, the bread of sincerity and truth."

6. How should the Corinthians have responded to the immorality in their midst?

7. Paul rebuked the church at Corinth for becoming arrogant. Why would arrogance keep them from dealing with the situation appropriately?

_____

_____

8. We are not to follow teachings contrary to God's Word or tolerate professing Christians who do so. How does Paul instruct Titus in Titus 3:9–11 concerning those who are teaching falsehood and undermining the faith?

> **3:9** "But avoid foolish controversies, genealogies, quarrels, and fights about the law, because they are useless and empty. **3:10** Reject a divisive person after one or two warnings. **3:11** You know that such a person is twisted by sin and is conscious of it himself."

_____

_____

9. Jesus rebuked the church at Pergamum for tolerating those who, like Balaam, undermined people's faith. For what faith-undermining ideas and practices do we need to be on the lookout?

_____

_____

10. In what ways does the world tempt us to compromise our integrity?

_____

_____

_____

11. Jesus rebuked the Pergamum church for tolerating those who followed false teaching that promoted idolatry and immorality. Instead,

they should have confronted those who taught such ideas. The church failed to practice church discipline. According to Matthew 18:15–18, what is the proper way to deal with sin in the midst of a church?

> **18:15** "If your brother sins, go and show him his fault when the two of you are alone. If he listens to you, you have regained your brother. **18:16** But if he does not listen, take one or two others with you, so that *at the testimony of two or three witnesses every matter may be established*. **18:17** If he refuses to listen to them, tell it to the church. If he refuses to listen to the church, treat him like a Gentile or a tax collector. **18:18** I tell you the truth, whatever you bind on earth will have been bound in heaven, and whatever you release on earth will have been released in heaven."

_____

_____

12. Why do you think many churches today, like the one in Pergamum, shy away from exercising corporate discipline?

_____

_____

13. Have you seen such discipline exercised in your church? If so, how was it handled and what happened afterward?

_____

_____

14. Earlier we discussed how we are not to judge. Yet here we are told God expects churches to deal with sin. How do we deal with sin without judging?

_____

_____

_____

15. High on God's priority list is for churches to hold to sound doctrine. Moral integrity is also essential. Are you aware of anyone around you who is teaching false doctrine?

_____

_____

_____

16. If so, what are they teaching and why is that false? How are you dealing with it?

_____

_____

_____

17. Are you "turning a blind eye" to someone in the church who is blatantly disobedient and compromising?

_____

18. Sit quietly before God and ask him to search your heart. Are you being influenced by false doctrine? Are you flirting with immorality? Are you tolerating things God hates? Do you need to take action?

THURSDAY: UNDERSTANDING GOD'S WILL

1. Pray for the Spirit to speak through his Word today; then read Jesus' words to the church at Pergamum from Revelation 2:16–17.

> **2:16** "Therefore, repent! If not, I will come against you quickly and make war against those people with the sword of my mouth. **2:17** The one who has an ear had better hear what the Spirit says to the churches. To the one who conquers, I will give him some of the hidden manna, and I will give him a white stone, and on that stone will be written a new name that no one can understand except the one who receives it."

2. What are Jesus' instructions to the church at Pergamum?

_____

_____

3. What is his warning, and what does it mean?

_____

_____

_____

4. Compare and contrast Jesus' instruction and warning to the Pergamum church (2:16) with his instruction and warning to the Ephesian church (2:5).

> **Rev. 2:5** "Therefore, remember from what high state you have fallen and repent! Do the deeds you did at the first; if not, I will come to you and remove your lampstand from its place—that is, if you do not repent."
>
> ·
>
> **Rev. 2:16** "Therefore, repent! If not, I will come against you quickly and make war against those people with the sword of my mouth."

_____

_____

_____

- *Repent* (2:5, 16). To repent means to change one's mind for the better, to heartily amend with abhorrence one's past sins—to "do a 180." It involves godly sorrow over our actions and a radical change of behavior. It means confessing and pleading for mercy. A great test of whether we're repentant is to consider, *If I had the whole thing to do over, would I choose to do it again? Or would I agree with God this time and run?* Repentance leaves no room for sinning with the knowledge that we'll later ask forgiveness.

5. Why were Jesus' warnings appropriate for each specific church (Ephesus and Pergamum) and its shortcomings?

_____

_____

_____

6. People choosing to follow the teachings of Balaam and the Nicolaitans were called to repent. Jesus called them to stop being corrupted by immorality and idolatry. In what ways do you see immorality and idolatry in the church today (no names, please)?

_____

_____

7. How do we as individuals and as a church balance being "in the world but not of the world" (see John 15:9)? That is, how can we influence the culture while still protecting ourselves from the world's way of thinking?

_____

_____

8. How is Paul's message to the Thessalonian church in 1 Thessalonians 4:1–8 similar to Jesus' message to the Pergamum church?

> **4:1** "Finally then, brothers and sisters, we ask you and urge you in the Lord Jesus, that as you received instruction from us about how you must live and please God (as you are in fact living) that you do so more and more. **4:2** For you know what commands we gave you through the Lord Jesus. **4:3** For this is God's will: that you become holy, that you keep away from sexual immorality, **4:4** that each of you know how to possess his own body in holiness and honor, **4:5** not in lustful passion like the Gentiles who do not know God. **4:6** In this matter no one should violate the rights of his brother or take advantage of him, because the Lord is the avenger in all these cases, as we also told you earlier and warned you solemnly. **4:7** For God did not call us to impurity but in holiness. **4:8** Consequently the

one who rejects this is not rejecting human authority but God, who gives his Holy Spirit to you."

_____

_____

9. According to 1 Thessalonians 4:3–7, what is God's will for the believer?

_____

• _Immorality_ (4:3). The word for _immorality_ used in addressing the church at Pergamum comes from the root _porneia_. Look familiar? Its meaning involves fornication or prostitution, and it differs from the word for _adultery_, which occurs later in Revelation 2, in that it does not necessarily involve violating a marriage bed. Interestingly, we find that when it comes to immorality in the Bible, rather than taking the usual approach to sin (arm ourselves and stand), we are told to flee! (See 1 Cor. 6:18.)

10. In Acts we read about a council of elders called together in Jerusalem to determine how to advise the Gentile believers in Christ about how they were to live. In the following passage you'll find the council's conclusions. What was their decision about things contaminated by idols and about immorality?

Acts 15:20 "We should write [Gentile converts] a letter telling them to abstain from things defiled by idols and from sexual immorality and from what has been strangled and from blood. **15:21** For Moses has had those who proclaim him in every town from ancient times, because he is read aloud in the synagogues every Sabbath."
. . . .

15:29 "That you abstain from meat that has been sacrificed to idols and from blood and from what has been strangled and from sexual immorality. If you keep yourselves from doing these things, you will do well. Farewell."

_____

_____

11. What steps can you take to guard yourself against immorality? (Think about how you dress, what you watch, where you go, who you hang out with, what you think about.)

_____

_____

12. Are there areas where you are embracing the world's values instead of what God values? If so, follow the instruction to the church at Pergamum: repent! Spend some time offering prayers of repentance, asking the Spirit to grant you the strength to live a sexually pure and holy life.

_____

_____

FRIDAY: OBEDIENCE HAS ITS REWARDS

1. Pray for spiritual insight; then read Jesus' warning to the church at Pergamum.

> **Rev. 2:17** "The one who has an ear had better hear what the Spirit says to the churches. To the one who conquers, I will give him some of the hidden manna, and I will give him a white stone, and on that stone will be written a new name that no one can understand except the one who receives it."

2. What three things did Jesus promise to the one who conquers?

_____

_____

• *Hidden manna* (2:17). One of the issues in Pergamum was eating literal food sacrificed to idols. Manna is set in direct contrast to this. The church was eating earthly pagan food, but the overcomer, or conqueror, is promised heavenly food from above.

3. We don't know for sure what the hidden manna refers to, but in light of John 6:31–35, 47–58, what is one possibility?

> **6:31** "Our ancestors ate the manna in the wilderness, just as it is written, *'He gave them bread from heaven to eat.'*

> **6:32** "Then Jesus told them, 'I tell you the solemn truth, it is not Moses who has given you the bread from heaven, but my Father is giving you the true bread from heaven. **6:33** For the bread of God is the one who comes down from heaven and gives life to the world.' **6:34** So they said to him, 'Sir, give us this bread all the time!'

> **6:35** "Jesus said to them, 'I am the bread of life. The one who comes to me will never go hungry, and the one who believes in me will never be thirsty.

> **6:47** "'I tell you the solemn truth, the one who believes has eternal life. **6:48** I am the bread of life. **6:49** Your ancestors ate the manna in the wilderness, and they died. **6:50** This is the bread that has come down from heaven, so that a person may eat from it and not die. **6:51** I am the living bread that came down from heaven. If anyone eats from this bread he will live forever. The bread that I will give for the life of the world is my flesh.'

> **6:52** "Then the Jews who were hostile to Jesus began to argue with one another, 'How can this man give us his flesh to eat?' **6:53** Jesus said to them, 'I tell you the solemn truth, unless you eat the flesh of the Son of Man and drink his blood, you have no life in yourselves. **6:54** The one who eats my flesh and drinks my blood has eternal life, and I will raise him up on the last day. **6:55** For my flesh is true food, and my blood is true drink. **6:56** The one who eats my flesh and drinks my blood resides in me, and I in him. **6:57** Just as the living Father sent me, and I live because of the Father, so the one who consumes me will live because of me. **6:58** This is the bread that came down from heaven; it is not like the bread your ancestors ate, but then later died. The one who eats this bread will live forever.'"

---

4. Scholars differ on the meaning of the white stone. This is perhaps the most difficult to interpret of all the rewards in Revelation 2 and 3. Among the many explanations are these:

A token of someone's innocence in a Greek court. A judge placed a white pebble in a ballot box when pronouncing a sentence of acquittal (a black pebble indicating condemnation).

A token of privilege. At Olympic games a victor's stone granted him special social privileges.

A token of initiation. Stones were used as tokens of initiation into the cult of Asklepios, which had a major presence in Pergamum. If this is what Jesus had in mind, he was co-opting a pagan symbol, redeeming it, and infusing it with his own meaning.

How might any of these explanations apply to a believer in a spiritual sense?

_____

_____

• *A white stone* (2:17). We find the only other biblical use of this word for stone in Acts 26:10. There we read where Paul tells Agrippa about his past persecution of Christians, and says that in Jerusalem, "Not only did I lock up many of the saints in prisons by the authority I received from the chief priests, but I also *cast my vote against them* when they were sentenced to death" (emphasis added). The phrase *cast my vote* is literally "cast down a pebble against them." A Greek idiom of the day was to "bring a pebble against someone," meaning to condemn in court. Here Paul uses the word to refer to voting against someone sentenced to death. Paul would have used a black stone in those situations. So one possible meaning of *white stone* here is that God promises to acquit of sin. Yet Strabo, the ancient Greek geographer, offers us another possibility. He wrote, "And, among the other cities, Apameia [with whom the kingdom of Pergamum made a treaty in 188 B.C.] was often shaken by earthquakes. . . . The city was called Celaenae, [black] that is, after Celaenus, the son of Poseidon by Celaeno, one of the daughters of Danaüs, or else because of the "blackness" of the stone, which resulted from the burn-outs.[12]

With earthquakes come fires. So black burned stone possibly reminded citizens of the instability and terror brought by constant shifts in the landscape. Possibly the white stone represented security.

[12] Strabo, *Geography* 12.18.

5. That white stone has writing on it—a new name inscribed. Scholars also differ on the meaning of "a new name. "In light of Isaiah 62:1–5 and 65:15, what might be one possibility?

> **62:1** "For the sake of Zion I will not be silent;
> for the sake of Jerusalem I will not be quiet,
> until her vindication shines brightly
> and her deliverance burns like a torch.
> **62:2** Nations will see your vindication,
> and all kings your splendor.
> You will be called by a new name
> that the Lord himself will give you.
> **62:3** You will be a majestic crown in the hand of the Lord,
> a royal turban in the hand of your God.
> **62:4** You will no longer be called, 'Abandoned,'
> and your land will no longer be called 'Desolate.'
> Indeed, you will be called 'My Delight is in Her,'
> and your land 'Married.'
> For the Lord will take delight in you,
> and your land will be married to him.
> **62:5** As a young man marries a young woman,
> so your sons will marry you.
> As a bridegroom rejoices over a bride,
> so your God will rejoice over you."

. . . .

> **65:15** "Your names will live on in the curse formulas of my chosen ones. The sovereign Lord will kill you, but he will give his servants another name."

---

6. In light of Revelation 22:3–4, what is another explanation?

> **22:3–4** "And there will no longer be any curse, and the throne of God and the Lamb will be in the city. His servants will worship him, and they will see his face, and his name will be on their foreheads."

Regardless of what we think about the identities of hidden manna and the white stone with a new name, one thing is certain. The promises revolve around the Lord Jesus Christ and make it worth whatever suffering believers must endure. In this life we might experience a small glimpse of God's promises about the future, but we won't grasp their fullness till we see Jesus face-to-face.

7. God provided the children of Israel with daily manna—literal food. Jesus called himself the bread of life—our spiritual food. What is the function of food? How does Christ nourish you and sustain you spiritually, both on a daily basis and eternally?

_____

_____

8. How do the three promises given to the one who conquers in Pergamum encourage you to view life from an eternal perspective rather than from a temporal, earthly perspective?

_____

_____

9. God gave new names to several people in the Bible. Remember that Saul was later called Paul (Acts 13:9) and Simon ("shifting sand") was renamed Peter ("stone") (John 1:41–42). Consider the following new names given in Genesis. Who were the people, what were their new names, and why were those names given? What promises did God give when he renamed these people?

> **17:5** "No longer will your name be Abram. Instead, your name will be Abraham because I will make you the father of a multitude of nations. **17:6** I will make you extremely fruitful. I will make nations of you, and kings will descend from you."
>
> . . . .
>
> **17:15** "Then God said to Abraham, 'As for your wife, you must no longer call her Sarai; 36 Sarah will be her name. **17:16** I will bless her and will give you a son through her. I will bless her and she will become a mother of nations. Kings of countries will come from her!'"
>
> . . . .

35:9 "God appeared to Jacob again after he returned from Paddan Aram and blessed him. **35:10** God said to him, 'Your name is Jacob, but your name will no longer be called Jacob; Israel will be your name.' So God named him Israel. **35:11** Then God said to him, 'I am the sovereign God. Be fruitful and multiply! A nation—even a company of nations—will descend from you; kings will be among your descendants! **35:12** The land I gave to Abraham and Isaac I will give to you. To your descendants I will also give this land.'"

Old Name	New Name	Why Given	Promise God Made

> "It is true that those we meet can change us, sometimes so profoundly that we are not the same afterwards, even unto our names. Witness Simon who is called Peter, Matthew also known as Levi, Nathaniel who is also Bartholomew, Judas—not Iscariot—who took the name Thaddeus, Simon who went by Niger, Saul who became Paul."—Yann Martel in *Life of Pi*

10. In the Book of Ruth, Naomi ("pleasant") told the people of Bethlehem to call her Mara ("bitter") after she lost her husband and both sons (Ruth 1:20). In Bible times, names often reflected one's character or circumstances. If God were to rename you a positive name based on your new character, what would you want him to name you and why? If you like to draw, sketch a drawing of a stone with your new name on it.

11. Reread the entire message to the church at Pergamum:

Rev. 2:12 To the angel of the church in Pergamum write the following:

"This is the solemn pronouncement of the one who has the sharp double-edged sword: **2:13** 'I know where you live—where Satan's throne is. Yet you continue to cling to my name and you have not denied your faith in me, even in the days of Antipas, my faithful witness, who was killed in your city where Satan lives. **2:14** But I have a few things against you: You have some people there who follow the teaching of Balaam, who instructed Balak to put a stumbling block before the people of Israel so they would eat food sacrificed to idols and commit sexual immorality. **2:15** In the same way, there are also some among you who follow the teaching of the Nicolaitans. **2:16** Therefore, repent! If not, I will come against you quickly and make war against those people with the sword of my mouth. **2:17** The one who has an ear had better hear what the Spirit says to the churches. To the one who conquers, I will give him some of the hidden manna, and I will give him a white stone, and on that stone will be written a new name that no one can understand except the one who receives it.'"

Here are some lessons we learn from the message to this church:

- Behind all false religion is Satan.
- It's unnecessary to have religious freedom to be found faithful.
- We must never judge the future by the present.
- God punishes sin but lavishly rewards those who are loyal in body and spirit.
- God seeks followers who refuse to compromise.
- Justice will someday reign.

12. When you read that justice will someday reign, does that give you hope or frighten you? Why?

_____

_____

_____

The Pergamum church faced the same choice that every church faces. They could compromise and face the terror of Jesus Christ's judgment. Or they could repent and receive unimaginable blessings.

_____

_____

I didn't expect Pergamum to take my breath away. To get there we drove through the fertile Caicus valley, fifteen miles inland, to the city of Bergma. Then we wound our way up the mountain against which the modern town is nestled. And from the top looking down, we drank in the miles of terraces, lush fields, and orchards.

For more than twenty-five years beautiful Pergamum served as the capital of Asia Minor, but it was also an important religious center. And as we gazed down and around at Pergamum's buildings, we saw a city patterned after the Athens Acropolis. Numerous remains hinted at Pergamum's former grandeur. It has been said that the Greeks built temples and the Romans built arches. Pergamum's structures stand as monuments to both.

We saw the arches of an aqueduct on the hillside below, pillars that once lined opulent streets, and a steep marble V-shaped theater that once held ten thousand people. Then there was the library that at its height contained two hundred thousand works. Antony gave it to Cleopatra as a gift, and the people in Alexandria, Egypt, fearing that the Pergamum library might exceed their own, stopped selling books to Asia. According to our archeologist/architect guide, the people of Pergamum responded by developing their own form of paper. In fact, the city derives its name from the ancient word for *parchment*.

Something struck me as sad about that library, though. Citizens could access it only by passing first through a temple to Athena, goddess of wisdom. That probably left Christians—who followed the one called Holy Wisdom—at a cultural disadvantage.

More troubling, though, were the foundational remains of a huge temple to Zeus, king of the gods in the Greek pantheon. Though the Germans have toted to Berlin much of the temple's contents, the site was still prominent.

Jesus Christ's church in the city of Pergamum lived in the midst of a paganism unlike anywhere else. People there worshiped at the temples of Zeus and Athena, and they also traveled to Pergamum as the center of Aesculapius worship. Aesculapius was the Greek god of healing, whose symbol was a serpent. (We still recognize that image as the caduceus, the medical symbol, with a staff entwined with serpents.) And as if that weren't enough, within one hundred years after

John recorded his vision, the Romans went on to erect a temple there to the emperor.

When we hear about such places immersed in pagan culture, it's easy to think we have little in common with them. Nobody has erected worship centers to honor Harry Truman or Gerald Ford. We don't pass through temples to get to the public library.

Yet like the Christians at Pergamum, we do live in a time when false religions scream against Jesus Christ's exclusive claims. It's cool to be spiritual, but not if it breeds the kind of so-called intolerance that says Jesus is the way, the truth, and the life, and that no one comes to the Father except through him (see John 14:6). It's fine to go to church until people find out its teachings include the idea that a man shouldn't lie with a man. And what single person wants to admit, "I'm a virgin." Or say, "No, I won't spend the night even if you promise to keep your hands where they belong, because I need to flee temptation and avoid the appearance of evil." People say, "Whatever works for you"—until we disagree with a popular talk-show host whose words contradict the Bible. Then our religion doesn't "work" because we're infringing on "her truth."

We do need to be winsome. We must listen to and engage the culture and care. Christians need to have a reputation for love as much as for truth. But in the end we also have to stand firm. In fact, our greatest danger lies less in the culture's antagonistic view of Christianity than in the fact that believers fear people more than God.

The church at Pergamum had issues with compromising. And Jesus' warning to them applies as much today as at any time in history.

Do you remain silent when you should speak? Do you sound like everyone around you, or are you taking a stand? What is your faith costing you? How much are you willing to spend? Who is your God, and is he worth the sacrifice?

Pray: Almighty Father in heaven, thank you for sending your Son, who was and who is and who is coming. Thank you for being a great God. I exist by your power and for your glory. Lord, I dedicate to you my life. You are worthy! By your grace, help me to be a witness in the place where you've put me. Use me as an instrument to influence people to worship you. Help me stand strong in this generation, to refuse to be squeezed into the world's mold, despite the pressure. Do this all for the glory of your name so the world will know that Christ alone is Lord. In his name I pray. Amen.

Memorize: "Therefore, repent! If not, I will come against you quickly and make war against those people with the sword of my mouth. The one who has an ear had better hear what the Spirit says to the churches. To the one who conquers, I will give him some of the hidden manna, and I will give him a white stone, and on that stone will be written a new name that no one can understand except the one who receives it'" (Rev. 2:16–17).

WEEK 5 OF 8

Thyatira: The Tolerant Church
Revelation 2:18–29

Scripture: "I will repay each one of you what your deeds deserve" (Rev. 2:23).

At a job interview, we might respond to inquiries like these: "Are you willing to work weekends? Are you OK with being on call one Saturday per month?" Yet imagine if every potential employer asked you this: "Do you worship the sun god? Are you willing to do so daily as part of membership in our guild?" Christ-followers would have to start our own businesses, wouldn't we? But what if clients refused to come into our stores unless we repented of our "atheism"?

Such a scenario gives us a little glimpse into life for followers of The Way in ancient Thyatira.

Luke identifies Lydia, Paul's first convert in Philippi, as "a dealer in purple cloth" from Thyatira (Acts 16:14). Apparently the city had ideal waters for fabric dyeing with a special reputation for producing *purple*—a word that in Luke's day included a broad range of reds.

Pilgrims arriving in the present-day Anatolian Turkish city of Akhisar (pronounced ahk-hee-SAHR) will find no remains lying on the ground from the first-century city of Thyatira, though the former city was built atop the latter. Yet with a little digging, we've found that while most first-century cities sat perched on hills, Thyatira lay on a flat plain with no city walls. It was the smallest of the seven cities mentioned in Revelation, sitting at the intersection of minor trade routes. And it had a long history of changing hands frequently because of its prime location and lack of natural and man-made protections.

As in the rest of Asia, Thyatira's citizens worshiped many gods. But the city's main deity was Apollo, the sun god, also called Tyrimnas.[13] He was represented with flaming rays and feet of burnished brass. At one time Thyatira was even considered a holy city because it housed a temple to Tyrimnas and held games in his honor. Early coins depict him on a horse, wielding a double-headed battle-ax.[14]

Ancient remains tell us something else that's significant about the city. Inscriptions dating back to Vespasian (about AD 69) and Marcus Aurelius Antoninus (about AD 211), mention corporate guilds.[15] Thyatira's trade guilds were probably more organized than in any other ancient city, and every serious artisan belonged to one. All guilds were incorporated organizations possessing property, making contracts, and exerting wide influence. This made it nearly impossible to survive economically apart from guild membership. It would be like a private mom-and-pop store trying to compete for the same bulk discounts offered to Walmart.

The church in Thyatira received lavish commendations from the Lord, yet some of its members followed false teaching. Many experts think the false teachers encouraged believers to join the trade guilds.[16] Doing so would have involved participating in pagan practices such as worship, eating food sacrificed to idols at union feasts, and sexual immorality. This, then, was probably the church's vital flaw: they tolerated the ideas of someone undermining true, whole-hearted commitment to God.

[13] *The New Unger's Bible Dictionary.* Originally published by Moody Press of Chicago, Illinois, 1988.
[14] International Standard Bible Encyclopaedia, Bible Works 4.0 CD-ROM, "Thyatira."
[15] Fausset's Bible Dictionary, Electronic Database, 1998, Biblesoft.
[16] George Raymond Beasley-Murray. *The Book of Revelation.* New Century Bible Commentary Series (Grand Rapids: Eerdmans Publishing Co., 1983), 89-90.

"Sure, you can join a god-worshiping guild, as long as you honor Christ in your heart." Can't you just hear it?

"God doesn't expect you to starve, does he?"

"Don't be such a separatist. How can you influence pagans if you refuse to work with them?"

Sometimes the pressure of "making it" and getting ahead and fitting in overwhelms us. As my friend Lance says, sometimes "my hope is built on nothing less than MasterCard and American Express." Yet the message to Thyatira reminds us that we must stand firm in our faith, refusing to compromise, trusting God to take care of us, and being willing to sacrifice all, if that's what it takes to follow. Do you believe God will supply your true needs? Are you willing to trust him even when it costs you something?

MONDAY: OUR HEAVENLY KNOW-IT-ALL

1. Pray for the Spirit to grant you insight; then read Revelation 2:18–28:

Rev. 2:18 "To the angel of the church in Thyatira write the following:

"This is the solemn pronouncement of the Son of God, the one who has eyes like a fiery flame and whose feet are like polished bronze: **2:19** 'I know your deeds: your love, faith, service, and steadfast endurance. In fact, your more recent deeds are greater than your earlier ones. **2:20** But I have this against you: You tolerate that woman Jezebel, who calls herself a prophetess, and by her teaching deceives my servants to commit sexual immorality and to eat food sacrificed to idols. **2:21** I have given her time to repent, but she is not willing to repent of her sexual immorality. **2:22** Look! I am throwing her onto a bed of violent illness, and those who commit adultery with her into terrible suffering, unless they repent of her deeds. **2:23** Furthermore, I will strike her followers with a deadly disease, and then all the churches will know that I am the one who searches minds and hearts. I will repay each one of you what your deeds deserve. **2:24** But to the rest of you in Thyatira, all who do not hold to this teaching (who have not learned the so-called "deep secrets of Satan"), to you I say: I do not put any additional burden on you. **2:25** However, hold on to what you have until I come. **2:26** And to the one who conquers and who continues in my deeds until the end, I will give him authority over the nations—

2:27 *he will rule them with an iron rod*
and like clay jars he will break them to pieces,

2:28 just as I have received the right to rule from my Father—and I will give him the morning star. **2:29** The one who has an ear had better hear what the Spirit says to the churches.'"

2. In this message, what description of Jesus do you find?

_____

_____

What commendation for the church?

_____

_____

What criticism?

_____

_____

What consequence and exhortation?

_____

_____

What promise to the one who conquers?

_____

_____

_____

Use your answers to fill in the chart at the beginning of this book. Also locate Thyatira on the map.

3. Describe your overall impression of the church at Thyatira.

_____

_____

4. In Jesus' message to the church at Thyatira, we find the only instance in Revelation where the expression *Son of God* appears.[17] What does this name suggest, and what are some possible reasons Jesus uses it with this church alone?

_____

_____

5. Jesus Christ is described in 2:18 as "the Son of God, the one who has eyes like a fiery flame and whose feet are like burnished bronze." (See also 1:14–15.) Fiery eyes suggest discerning and severe judgment. *Burnished* means "highly reflective."[18] Why might this description of Christ be appropriate for this specific church?

_____

_____

6. We don't know who founded the church at Thyatira. But Luke records something about a woman from Thyatira living in Philippi when Paul goes there to spread the gospel. According to Acts 16:14, who is from Thyatira, and what do we learn about her?

> 16:14 "A woman named Lydia, a dealer in purple cloth from the city of Thyatira, a God-fearing woman, listened to us. The Lord opened her heart to respond to what Paul was saying."

_____

_____

_____

---

[17] Kenneth L. Barker, *The Expositor's Bible Commentary, 1146.*
[18] Tom Constable, *Expository Notes on Revelation [CD-ROM], 33.*

7. In Revelation 2:19, what does Jesus say he knows about the church at Thyatira?

_____

_____

8. Note Jesus' first words in this message: "I know." What do we learn about God's all-knowing character from this verse as well as the following passages?

Gen. 16:13 "So Hagar named the Lord who spoke to her, 'You are the God who sees me,' for she said, 'Here I have seen one who sees me!'"

. . . .

Jer. 11:20 "So I said to the Lord, 'O Lord who rules over all, you are a just judge! You examine people's hearts and minds. I want to see you pay them back for what they have done because I trust you to vindicate my cause.'"

. . . .

Jer. 17:9–10 "The human mind is more deceitful than anything else. It is incurably bad. Who can understand it? 17:10 I, the Lord, probe into people's minds. I examine people's hearts. I deal with each person according to how he has behaved. I give them what they deserve based on what they have done."

. . . .

Jer. 20:12 "O Lord who rules over all, you test and prove the righteous. You see into people's hearts and minds. Pay them back for what they have done because I trust you to vindicate my cause."

. . . .

Acts 1:24 "Then they prayed, 'Lord, you know the hearts of all. Show us which one of these two you have chosen . . .'"

. . . .

Acts 15:8 "And God, who knows the heart, has testified to them by giving them the Holy Spirit just as he did to us . . ."

_____

_____

_____

9. In what circumstances in your life do you find comfort in knowing God sees and knows your heart? In what does that truth bring anxiety?

_____

_____

10. Read Psalm 139:1–16; then list the ways in which the psalmist indicates God sees and knows him.

> **139:1** "O Lord, you examine me and know.
> **139:2** You know when I sit down and when I get up;
> even from far away you understand my motives.
> **139:3** You carefully observe me when I travel or when I lie
>   down to rest;
> you are aware of everything I do.
> **139:4** Certainly my tongue does not frame a word
> without you, O Lord, being thoroughly aware of it.
> **139:5** You squeeze me in from behind and in front;
> you place your hand on me.
> **139:6** Your knowledge is beyond my comprehension;
> it is so far beyond me, I am unable to fathom it.
> **139:7** Where can I go to escape your spirit?
> Where can I flee to escape your presence?
> **139:8** If I were to ascend to heaven, you would be there.
> If I were to sprawl out in Sheol, there you would be.
> **139:9** If I were to fly away on the wings of the dawn,
> and settle down on the other side of the sea,
> **139:10** even there your hand would guide me,
> your right hand would grab hold of me.
> **139:11** If I were to say, 'Certainly the darkness will cover me,
> and the light will turn to night all around me,'
> **139:12** even the darkness is not too dark for you to see,
> and the night is as bright as day;
> darkness and light are the same to you.
> **139:13** Certainly you made my mind and heart;
> you wove me together in my mother's womb.
> **139:14** I will give you thanks because your deeds are
>   awesome and amazing.
> You knew me thoroughly;
> **139:15** my bones were not hidden from you,
> when I was made in secret

and sewed together in the depths of the earth.
139:16 Your eyes saw me when I was inside the womb.
All the days ordained for me
were recorded in your scroll
before one of them came into existence.

---

11. One group of believers might have a great reputation in the community or within the body of Christ. Another group garners little respect, or it is discounted because of its small size. Yet Jesus' penetrating eyes see each group as it truly is. This truth should keep us humble when we're praised, and keep us persevering when we feel overlooked. As God searches your heart and mind today, what does he find? On what does your heart and mind dwell?

---

12. List areas where you feel people respect you or your church, but you know of problems they don't know about (no names, please).

---

13. As God looks with his penetrating eyes that see all things, do you think he's disappointed with your church? With you? If so, why or why not?

---

1. Read Revelation 2:18–19:

> **2:18** To the angel of the church in Thyatira write the following:
>
> "This is the solemn pronouncement of the Son of God, the one who has eyes like a fiery flame and whose feet are like polished bronze: **2:19** 'I know your deeds: your love, faith, service, and steadfast endurance. In fact, your more recent deeds are greater than your earlier ones.'"

2. For what did Jesus commend Thyatira and why are these qualities so vital to spiritual growth?

_____

_____

3. Compare and contrast Jesus' praise for Thyatira with his commendation for the church at Ephesus:

> **Revelation 2:1** To the angel of the church in Ephesus, write the following:
>
> "This is the solemn pronouncement of the one who has a firm grasp on the seven stars in his right hand—the one who walks among the seven golden lampstands: **2:2** 'I know your works as well as your labor and steadfast endurance, and that you cannot tolerate evil. You have even put to the test those who refer to themselves as apostles (but are not), and have discovered that they are false. **2:3** I am also aware that you have persisted steadfastly, endured much for the sake of my name, and have not grown weary.'"

_____

_____

4. What similarities with the commendation to Thyatira do you see in Paul's exhortation to Timothy (1 Tim. 6:11–12)?

> **6:11** "But you, as a person dedicated to God, keep away from all that. Instead pursue righteousness, godliness, faithfulness, love, endurance, and gentleness. **6:12** Compete well for the faith and lay

hold of that eternal life you were called for and made your good confession for in the presence of many witnesses."

---

5. How do the qualities of love, faith, service, and perseverance relate to one another?

---

6. In which of these qualities are you the strongest? the weakest?

---

7. In what ways can you cooperate with God to strengthen where you are weakest?

---

8. How does Paul's commendation of the Colossian church in Colossians 1:3–8 compare to the commendation of the church at Thyatira?

1:3 "We always give thanks to God, the Father of our Lord Jesus Christ, when we pray for you, **1:4** since we heard about your faith in Christ Jesus and the love that you have for all the saints. **1:5** Your faith and love have arisen from the hope laid up for you in heaven, which you have heard about in the message of truth, the gospel **1:6** that has come to you. Just as in the entire world this gospel is bearing fruit and growing, so it has also been bearing fruit and growing among you from the first day you heard it and understood the grace of God in truth. **1:7** You learned the gospel from Epaphras, our dear fellow slave—a faithful minister of Christ on our behalf—**1:8** who also told us of your love in the Spirit."

---

9. In 2 Peter 1:1–9, what qualities does Peter encourage believers to pursue and why?

1:1 "From Simeon Peter, a slave and apostle of Jesus Christ, to those who through the righteousness of our God and Savior, Jesus Christ, have been granted a faith just as precious as ours. **1:2** May grace and peace be lavished on you as you grow in the rich knowledge of God and of Jesus our Lord! **1:3** I can pray this because his divine power has bestowed on us everything necessary for life and godliness through the rich knowledge of the one who called us by his own glory and excellence. **1:4** Through these things he has bestowed on us his precious and most magnificent promises, so that by means of what was promised you may become partakers of the divine nature, after escaping the worldly corruption that is produced by evil desire. **1:5** For this very reason, make every effort to add to your faith excellence, to excellence, knowledge; **1:6** to knowledge, self-control; to self-control, perseverance; to perseverance, godliness; **1:7** to godliness, brotherly affection; to brotherly affection, unselfish love. **1:8** For if these things are really yours and are continually increasing, they will keep you from becoming ineffective and unproductive in your pursuit of knowing our Lord Jesus Christ more intimately. **1:9** But concerning the one who lacks such things—he is blind. That is to say, he is nearsighted, since he has forgotten about the cleansing of his past sins."

---

10. Pray for yourself in the areas that are important to the Lord, according to his Word.

11. Sometimes in our relationships with God, we focus only on our failures. Yet in most of his messages to the seven churches, Jesus also includes positive assessments. Rather than focusing only on what's wrong, consider what's going well. In what ways do you see progress and growth in your walk with God and in your character as a result?

_____

_____

12. Thank the Lord for all he is doing in your life. If you feel you've stopped moving forward in your spiritual walk, talk honestly with God and ask him to rekindle the fire.

13. Remember that Jesus' assessments of the churches were evaluations of groups, not individuals. What is one way you can help your own local assembly of believers to move forward in love, faith, service, and endurance?

_____

_____

WEDNESDAY: THE HEART-SEARCHER

1. Pray for the Spirit to grant you insight as you study God's Word; then read Revelation 2:20–23.

> **2:20** "But I have this against you: You tolerate that woman Jezebel, who calls herself a prophetess, and by her teaching deceives my servants to commit sexual immorality and to eat food sacrificed to idols. **2:21** I have given her time to repent, but she is not willing to repent of her sexual immorality. **2:22** Look! I am throwing her onto a bed of violent illness, and those who commit adultery with her into terrible suffering, unless they repent of her deeds. **2:23** Furthermore, I will strike her followers with a deadly disease, and then all the churches will know that I am the one who searches minds and hearts. I will repay each one of you what your deeds deserve."

2. Circle all the references to sexual immorality, adultery, and bed.

3. What is Jesus' criticism of the church at Thyatira, and how does it compare or contrast with his criticism of the church at Pergamum in Revelation 2:14–15?

> **2:14** "But I have a few things against you: You have some people there who follow the teaching of Balaam, who instructed Balak to put a stumbling block before the people of Israel so they would eat food sacrificed to idols and commit sexual immorality. **2:15** In the same way, there are also some among you who follow the teaching of the Nicolaitans."

---

4. What does the message to the church at Thyatira tell us about Jezebel?

---

5. In *Women in the World of the Earliest Christians*, Lynn Cohick writes, "It is not entirely clear whether the person responsible for the false teachings is female, as one method of denigrating a male opponent is to liken him to a woman. Nonetheless, given the other examples of women instructing the church, this 'Jezebel' could be a historical woman. If this is the case, we can be reasonably certain that she did not self-identify as Jezebel; rather, John indicted her character and teachings by connecting her with the infamous Jezebel of Israel's past who tormented and killed God's prophets."[19] That is, Jezebel in the church at Thyatira most likely is a euphemistic label given because of similarities to the Jezebel in the Old Testament. What do we know about the Old Testament Jezebel from these passages?

> **1 Kings 16:30–31** "Ahab son of Omri did more evil in the sight of the Lord than all who were before him. As if following in the sinful footsteps of Jeroboam son of Nebat were not bad enough, he

---

[19] Lynn Cohick. *Women in the World of the Earliest Christians: Illuminating Ancient Ways of Life.* (Grand Rapids, Michigan: Baker Academic, 2009)

married Jezebel the daughter of King Ethbaal of the Sidonians. Then he worshiped and bowed to Baal."

- -

1 Kings 18:4 "When Jezebel was killing the Lord's prophets, Obadiah took one hundred prophets and hid them in two caves in two groups of fifty. He also brought them food and water."

- -

1 Kings 18:19 "Now send out messengers and assemble all Israel before me at Mount Carmel, as well as the 450 prophets of Baal and 400 prophets of Asherah whom Jezebel supports."

- -

1 Kings 19:1–2 "Ahab told Jezebel all that Elijah had done, including a detailed account of how he killed all the prophets with the sword. Jezebel sent a messenger to Elijah with this warning, 'May the gods judge me severely if by this time tomorrow I do not take your life as you did theirs!'"

- -

1 Kings 21:25–26 "(There had never been anyone like Ahab, who was firmly committed to doing evil in the sight of the Lord, urged on by his wife Jezebel. He was so wicked he worshiped the disgusting idols, just like the Amorites whom the Lord had driven out from before the Israelites.)"

- -

2 Kings 9:22 "When Jehoram saw Jehu, he asked, 'Is everything all right, Jehu?' He replied, 'How can everything be all right as long as your mother Jezebel promotes idolatry and pagan practices?'"

---

6. How is the Old Testament Jezebel similar to the Jezebel described in Revelation?

Both Balaam and Jezebel in Revelation may represent groups rather than individuals. Note that both a male and female are included in the indictments, with neither men nor women presented as more likely to adhere to false teaching. The Old Testament story about Jezebel describes her as one who influenced others to engage in idolatry, not someone who committed literal adultery. In the Old Testament, writers presented idolatry and infidelity to God using sexual metaphors such as adultery and prostitution. The entire Book of Hosea is the story of a prophet's prostitute wife used by God to picture Israel's behavior toward him. Later in Revelation, Jesus condemns idolatry using sexual immorality as a metaphor (Rev. 17:2; 18:3). So while it's possible the Jezebel in Thyatira was a lone woman who encouraged literal sexual immorality, it seems equally likely that "she" was a group of believers who counseled others to be unfaithful to God by compromising in a pagan environment.

7. What does the text say will happen to the Jezebel in Thyatira and those who follow her if she continues in her unrepentant state?

_____

_____

• *Bed of violent illness* (2:22). The Greek word translated *bed* here means simply a cot or stretcher. But the translators have caught the Old Testament idea behind being on a bed and qualified it with "violent illness," just as today when we say someone is in bed, we mean sick or injured. To throw someone onto a bed, then, means to inflict the person with suffering. Notice that those sinning in Thyatira go from a bed of adultery to a bed of suffering. The place remains the same, but the pleasure turns to pain.

8. Notice that Jesus holds out hope even for someone like Jezebel. He says he will act in judgment *if* she does not repent. What hope does this suggest for her if she *does* repent?

_____

_____

9. What does this tell us about God's grace toward those who repent?

_____

_____

10. What is the purpose in God's judgment on Jezebel, and why is that important?

_____

_____

11. Some in Thyatira tolerate Jezebel and engage in the sin she condones. How do you think a believer gets to that point where he or she listens to such false teaching?

_____

_____

12. If Jezebel refused to repent, God promised consequences. Paul addressed repentance in Romans 2:4–11. List the attributes of God in this passage and how they relate to repentance.

> **2:4** "Or do you have contempt for the wealth of his kindness, forbearance, and patience, and yet do not know that God's kindness leads you to repentance? **2:5** But because of your stubbornness and your unrepentant heart, you are storing up wrath for yourselves in the day of wrath, when God's righteous judgment is revealed! **2:6** He **_will reward each one according to his works:_** **2:7** eternal life to those who by perseverance in good works seek glory and honor and immortality, **2:8** but wrath and anger to those who live in selfish ambition and do not obey the truth but follow unrighteousness. **2:9** There will be affliction and distress on everyone who does evil, on the Jew first and also the Greek, **2:10** but glory and honor and peace for everyone who does good, for the Jew first and also the Greek. **2:11** For there is no partiality with God."

_____

13. What are the end results for one with an unrepentant heart?

_____

_____

14. Are you influencing another believer to violate his or her conscience in any way?

_____

_____

_____

15. Ask God to search your heart. Are there areas where you feel the Spirit urging you to change, yet you continue to resist?

_____

_____

_____

Questions for Self-Evaluation

Materialism. Am I giving sacrificially to support God's work and meet others' needs?

Prayer. Am I creating space to talk with God and listen to his "still, small voice"?

Forgiveness. Am I seeking forgiveness from those I've wronged? And am I offering forgiveness to those who have wronged me or others?

Community. Am I regularly engaging in accountable relationships, engaging in corporate worship, and sitting under biblical teaching?

Fasting. Do I need to abstain from food to get a handle on my cravings and create more space for God in my life?

Time and affections. Are my time and energy focused on what matters? Do I tolerate my own unhealthy attachments to shopping, food, Internet, television, computer time, movies, books, or individuals?

Listening. Do I sense the Spirit urging me in some way, and am I responding as he directs?

16. End your time in prayer today with the Lord's Prayer (Matt. 6:9–15). "Our Father. . . ."

THURSDAY: HOLD ON!

1. Pray for the Spirit to enlighten you; then read Revelation 2:24–25:

> **2:24** "But to the rest of you in Thyatira, all who do not hold to this teaching (who have not learned the so-called 'deep secrets of Satan'), to you I say: I do not put any additional burden on you. **2:25** However, hold on to what you have until I come."

2. What is Jesus' instruction to the faithful remnant in the church at Thyatira?

_____

_____

3. How does Jesus describe those who reject Jezebel's false teaching?

_____

_____

- *'Deep secrets' of Satan* (2:24). There are several possibilities for what this phrase means. By refusing to participate in pagan trade guilds, Christ-followers were excluded from the intricacies of pagan practice—practices that could be synonymous with the deep secrets. So these secrets could be the deep knowledge of idol worship. It's also possible Jesus means something less literal here. Both those who followed Balaam's teaching and those who followed Jezebel's teaching had something in common—they compromised. Sometimes we might think we're doing OK if we aren't experiencing spiritual blowouts, yet the less-discernable slow leaks lead to the same result. Often Satan's methodology is to slowly wear us down, spiriting away larger and larger parts of our hearts until we eventually look and think like the world and those who deny Christ. So the deep secrets of Satan could be the ways in which Satan works to draw us away from Christ.

4. We looked at Ephesians 6:10–18 when we studied the letter to the church at Pergamum. Look at this passage again and describe the struggle we face.

> **6:10** "Finally, be strengthened in the Lord and in the strength of his power. **6:11** Clothe yourselves with the full armor of God so that you may be able to stand against the schemes of the devil. **6:12** For our struggle is not against flesh and blood, but against the rulers, against the powers, against the world rulers of this darkness, against the spiritual forces of evil in the heavens. **6:13** For this reason, take up the full armor of God so that you may be able to stand your ground on the evil day, and having done everything, to stand. **6:14** Stand firm therefore, by fastening the belt of truth around your waist, by putting on the breastplate of righteousness, **6:15** by fitting your feet with the preparation that comes from the good news of peace, **6:16** and in all of this, by taking up the shield of faith with which you can extinguish all the flaming arrows of the evil one. **6:17** And take the helmet of salvation and the sword of the Spirit, which is the word of God. **6:18** With every prayer and petition, pray at all times in the Spirit, and to this end be alert, with all perseverance and requests for all the saints."

_____

_____

5. What are some lies that the world and the evil one convey to us that are contrary to God's truth? Why do you think we sometimes believe them?

_____

_____

6. In what ways have you experienced spiritual warfare? How have you overcome it?

_____

_____

_____

7. How can we "hold on" to what we have until Jesus comes?

_____

_____

8. Jesus tells those in Thyatira to hold on. What do the following verses tell us about holding on?

Deuteronomy 11:22–23 "For if you carefully observe all of these commandments I am giving you and love the Lord your God, live according to his standards, and remain loyal to him, then he will drive out all these nations ahead of you, and you will dispossess nations greater and stronger than you."

. . . .

1 Corinthians 15:1–2 "Now I want to make clear for you, brothers and sisters, the gospel that I preached to you, that you received and on which you stand, and by which you are being saved, if you hold firmly to the message I preached to you—unless you believed in vain."

. . . .

1 Timothy 6:12 "Compete well for the faith and lay hold of that eternal life you were called for and made your good confession for in the presence of many witnesses."

. . . .

Hebrews 10:23 "And let us hold unwaveringly to the hope that we confess, for the one who made the promise is trustworthy."

_____

_____

_____

9. We might rephrase "Hold on" as "Keep doing what you're doing without wavering." Your labor is not in vain! What are you doing well that you need to persevere in?

_____

_____

10. In what areas does Satan tempt you to compromise?

_____

_____

11. Spend some time praying that God will grant you a fully loyal heart to follow him.

FRIDAY: HOPE THINKS ETERNAL

1. Pray that the Holy Spirit would move in your heart today and give you insight as you spend time in God's Word; then read Revelation 2:26–29:

> **Rev. 2:26** "'And to the one who conquers and who continues in my deeds until the end, I will give him authority over the nations—
>
> **2:27 _he will rule them with an iron rod_**
> **_and like clay jars he will break them to pieces,_***
>
> **2:28** just as I have received the right to rule from my Father—and I will give him the morning star. **2:29** The one who has an ear had better hear what the Spirit says to the churches.'"

2. In verse 26, Jesus begins to lay out the promises to the ones who conquer. What is different this time from all the previous messages to overcomers?

To Ephesus. "The one who has an ear had better hear what the Spirit says to the churches. To the one who conquers, I will permit him to eat from the tree of life that is in the paradise of God" (2:7).

To Smyrna. "The one who has an ear had better hear what the Spirit says to the churches. The one who conquers will in no way be harmed by the second death" (2:11).

To Pergamum. "The one who has an ear had better hear what the Spirit says to the churches. To the one who conquers, I will give him some of the hidden manna, and I will give him a white stone, and on that stone will be written a new name that no one can understand except the one who receives it" (2:17).

*Remember that verses in italics in the _NET Bible_ denote quotations from other places in Scripture.

To Thyatira. "And to the one who conquers and who continues in my deeds until the end, I will give him authority over the nations— *he will rule them with an iron rod and like clay jars he will break them to pieces,* just as I have received the right to rule from my Father—and I will give him the morning star. The one who has an ear had better hear what the Spirit says to the churches" (2:26–29).

_____

_____

3. Based on what you know about the situation in Thyatira, what are some possible reasons Jesus included these specific promises to that church?

_____

_____

_____

4. What two things does Jesus promise to the one who overcomes in Thyatira?

_____

_____

5. According to Revelation 5:10; 20:4–6; 22:5, what does it mean that he will give them authority and they will rule?

> **5:10** "You have appointed them as a kingdom and priests to serve our God, and they will reign on the earth."

. . . .

> **20:4–6** "Then I saw thrones and seated on them were those who had been given authority to judge. I also saw the souls of those who had been beheaded because of the testimony about Jesus and because of the word of God. These had not worshiped the beast or his image and had refused to receive his mark on their forehead or hand. They came to life and reigned with Christ for a thousand years. (The rest of the dead did not come to life until the thousand years were finished.) This is the first resurrection. Blessed and holy

is the one who takes part in the first resurrection. The second death has no power over them, but they will be priests of God and of Christ, and they will reign with him for a thousand years."

....

22:5 "Night will be no more, and they will not need the light of a lamp or the light of the sun, because the Lord God will shine on them, and they will reign forever and ever."

"Many of us are paying more attention to the bad news according to cable TV than to the Good News according to Christ Jesus—to the *Wall Street Journal's* forecast than of God's sovereign hand in world affairs and His prophetic plan."—Dr. Charles Swindoll

6. In Revelation 2:28 Jesus promises the "morning star" to those who overcome (conquer). According to Revelation 22:16, who or what is the morning star?

22:16 "I, Jesus, have sent my angel to testify to you about these things for the churches. I am the root and the descendant of David, the bright morning star!"

• *The morning star* (Rev. 2:28). Venus, the second-closest planet to the sun, derives its name from the Roman goddess of love and beauty. The planet reaches its maximum brightness two times each day—shortly before sunrise or shortly after sunset; thus, it is often called the morning star or the evening star. Ancient Babylonian cuneiform texts identify it as early as fifteen centuries before Christ. The Babylonians called it Ishtar, the personification of womanhood and goddess of love. The Greeks named it after their goddess of love, Aphrodite. And by John's day, the Romans had named the planet Venus after their own goddess of love.

Pliny the Elder, a first-century author and natural philosopher, says this about the planet: "Beneath the sun a goodly fair star there is, called Venus, which goes her compass, wandering this way and that, by turns: and by the very names that it has, testifies to her emulation of sun and moon. . . . She takes the name of *Lucifer* (or *Daystar*) as a second sun hastening the day. . . . Now this planet, in greatness, goes beyond all the other five: and it is so clear and shining that the beams of this one star cast shadows on the earth. And herein lies the great diversity and ambiguity of its names: some have called it Juno, others Isis, and others the Mother of the gods."[20] However we look at it, by the time John recorded Jesus' revelation to him, the planet had a long tradition of associations with pagan love gods. But in Revelation the name is attributed to the one true God—the Lord Jesus Christ. By referring to himself as both the descendant of David and as the morning star, Jesus was speaking in a language understood by both Jews and Gentiles.

7. Jesus promises that the overcomer will be given "the morning star" (2:28), and elsewhere we learn that Jesus himself *is* the morning star. So what is he promising? And why does this offer fabulous hope for Thyatira's believers, who have virtually nothing?

_____

_____

8. Consider how Jesus takes the glory false gods stole from him and reclaims that glory for himself. Daystar was a name with pagan associations. Instead of distancing himself from that name, Jesus reveals himself as the true Daystar. What does this suggest about how Christ-followers can infuse cultural symbols and practices with redemptive meaning?

_____

_____

9. In Revelation 2:26–27, Jesus quotes Psalm 2, a Messianic psalm telling how the Father gave the Messiah authority over the nations.

[20] Pliny the Elder, *Natural History*, ii,8.

The New Testament writers frequently quote this psalm and apply it to Jesus Christ as the great Son of David and God's anointed one. What do you learn about his future reign from the following passages?

Psalm 2

Psa. 2:1 Why do the nations rebel? Why are the countries devising plots that will fail?

2:2 The kings of the earth form a united front; the rulers collaborate against the Lord and his anointed king.

2:3 They say, "Let's tear off the shackles they've put on us! Let's free ourselves from their ropes!"

2:4 The one enthroned in heaven laughs in disgust; the Lord taunts them.

2:5 Then he angrily speaks to them and terrifies them in his rage, saying,

2:6 "I myself have installed my king on Zion, my holy hill."

2:7 The king says, 'I will announce the Lord's decree. He said to me: "You are my son! This very day I have become your father!

2:8 Ask me, and I will give you the nations as your inheritance, the ends of the earth as your personal property.

2:9 You will break them with an iron scepter; you will smash them like a potter's jar!'

2:10 So now, you kings, do what is wise; you rulers of the earth, submit to correction!

2:11 Serve the Lord in fear! Repent in terror!

2:12 Give sincere homage! Otherwise he will be angry, and you will die because of your behavior, when his anger quickly ignites. How blessed are all who take shelter in him!

. . . .

Revelation 11:15–18

Rev. 11:15 Then the seventh angel blew his trumpet, and there were loud voices in heaven saying:

"The kingdom of the world has become the kingdom of our Lord and of his Christ, and he will reign for ever and ever."

11:16 Then the twenty-four elders who are seated on their thrones before God threw themselves down with their faces to the ground and worshiped God **11:17** with these words:

"We give you thanks, Lord God, the All-Powerful, the one who is and who was, because you have taken your great power and begun to reign.

11:18 The nations were enraged, but your wrath has come, and the time has come for the dead to be judged, and the time has come to give to your servants, the prophets, their reward, as well as to the saints and to those who revere your name, both small and great, and the time has come to destroy those who destroy the earth.'"

Revelation 19:11–16

Rev. 19:11 Then I saw heaven opened and here came a white horse! The one riding it was called "Faithful" and "True," and with justice he judges and goes to war. **19:12** His eyes are like a fiery flame and there are many diadem crowns on his head. He has a name written that no one knows except himself. **19:13** He is dressed in clothing dipped in blood, and he is called the Word of God. **19:14** The armies that are in heaven, dressed in white, clean, fine linen, were following him on white horses. **19:15** From his mouth extends a sharp sword, so that with it he can strike the nations. *He will rule them with an iron rod*, and he stomps the winepress of the furious wrath of God, the All-Powerful. **19:16** He has a name written on his clothing and on his thigh: "King of kings and Lord of lords."

> In Handel's *Messiah* the great composer set part of Psalm 2 to music in the aria, "Why Do the Nations?" In this and the "Hallelujah Chorus," we gain a sobering, magnificent view of our God as judge of the nations, as presented also in the Book of Revelation.

10. In your own words describe the ultimate future for the Christ-follower who perseveres.

11. How can "knowing how the story ends" affect how we view our present circumstances?

_____

_____

12. Spend a few moments expressing your worship of the great judge of all nations, the One who will conquer, the Morning Star.

13. Ask the Morning Star how your life can more fully reflect his radiance to the world. If you sense him speaking to you in some way, write about it here:

_____

_____

SATURDAY: NO COMPROMISE

"But I have this against you: You tolerate . . ." (Rev. 2:20).

Tolerance. Usually it's a good thing. We need it when it comes to gender conflict. And racial diversity. And interacting with people from other countries. We need to love those made different by God's design. On the nonessentials, we certainly need more grace. My daughter needs to tolerate my love for Jane Austen movies, and I need to tolerate her Justin Bieber mania. My friends tolerate their kids' tattoos and body piercings.

Yet sometimes tolerance is *not* a good thing. Sometimes we let our culture pressure us to tolerate what God hates. We even quote, "Judge not that you be not judged" (Matt. 7:1), using the Bible to justify our silence when we should speak up.

In the Book of Revelation, Jesus tells the church at Thyatira that what deeply offends him most is their tolerance. Instead of dealing with false teaching, they ignore it. And he hates that.

In the Sermon on the Mount, when Jesus told his followers not to judge, he followed up with an explanation: "You hypocrite. *First* remove the beam from your own eye, and *then* you can see clearly to remove the speck from your brother's eye" (Matt. 7:5, emphasis added). Note that he expects us to remove the speck—to deal with what was wrong. He just expects us to get rid of our own double standards first.

In 1 Corinthians 5:1–2, we read Paul's rebuke to the church at Corinth for putting up with a man sleeping with his father's wife. He says they should have kicked out this guy until he repented. Seems kind of judgmental, huh? Yup. That's exactly the kind of judgment Jesus wants us to have—we're to deal with the sin in our own lives and then guard the testimony of his followers. Now, notice Paul wasn't talking about an unbeliever acting in such a way. And in his message to Thyatira, Jesus isn't talking about confronting the pagans in Thyatira. His concern is for those who claim to know Christ yet accept the world's practices and ideas.

God's plan is for us to keep ourselves pure so we can have credibility to confront those teaching inside the body of Christ who teach what's false.

So if a sister in Christ whom I know well dresses immodestly, I need to pull her aside and encourage her to draw attention to her face instead of her body. But I can't do that if I'm standing there wearing a plunging neckline.

The false teachers in Thyatira were within the church, not outside. They may have even felt they were more spiritually mature than the rest. Paul described more-mature Christians in Corinth as being able to eat meat sacrificed to idols, as long as they didn't lead others to violate their consciences (see 1 Cor. 10). Years later, those in Thyatira seem to have taken such teaching too far. Perhaps they even considered themselves more free in the faith, thinking that the more we sin, the more we're covered by God's grace. If so, they missed the rest of Paul's teaching: "What shall we say then? Are we to remain in sin so that grace may increase? Absolutely not! How can we who died to sin still live in it?" (Rom. 6:1–2).

Most in the Thyatira church didn't buy such ideas. Yet they did nothing. They sat passively. They tolerated evil, failing to excise the ones propagating such lies.

Wrong approach.

Are you willing to be intolerant toward sin, which God hates, in the church? Are you learning what the Bible says so you can discern truth from falsehood? Are you living a pure life so you have the credibility to speak up when it counts?

Pray: Heavenly Father, in your image you made all people of the world. You made man and woman. You made different races. You made many tribes and nations and languages, and you scattered us throughout the world. To all of us you offer salvation through your Son Jesus Christ. Thank you for the diversity you made and your inclusiveness in making the gospel available to all.

But help us, our Father, to stand for the truth. Purify your church that we might declare your glory to the nations. Unify us and cleanse us and make us free of compromise. Help us to be gracious about unessential differences but intolerant about falsehood. Grant us the grace to follow you with undivided hearts, free from hypocrisy. Help us to think critically without becoming critics, to speak the truth without priding ourselves in our "great spirituality." Grant us that mix of tolerance and intolerance, that blend of love and justice, that you so desire in your followers. Please grant us the wisdom to know the difference. In the name of your Son, Amen.

Memorize: "However, hold on to what you have until I come. And to the one who conquers and who continues in my deeds until the end, I will give him authority over the nations" (Rev. 2:25–26).

WEEK 6 OF 8

Sardis: The Sleeping Church
Revelation 3:1–6

Scripture: "Therefore, remember what you received and heard, and obey it, and repent. If you do not wake up, I will come like a thief, and you will never know at what hour I will come against you" (Rev. 3:3).

Today a popular car-repair business advertises itself as having the Midas touch. The term has long described those who prosper in every endeavor. It comes from a popular Greek myth about King Midas, who turned everything he touched to gold. He couldn't enjoy human affection, however, because his "touch" turned people to gold too. The cure? Bathing in the Pactolus River that runs through Sardis.

What about the expression "as rich as Croesus"? Ever heard that? The wealthy Croesus, last king of Lydia—of which Sardis was the capital—lived from 560–546 BC. King Croesus panned for gold in the Pactolus and became the first monarch to mint coins. He helped finance the enormous temple to Artemis in Ephesus—one of the Seven Wonders of the Ancient World—and had a reputation for fantastic wealth.

Located about thirty miles south of Thyatira, Sardis sat atop a hill that towers fifteen hundred feet above a lush valley. Its height made the city feel secure, protected by nearly perpendicular "walls" on three sides. People entering Sardis could approach only by trudging up a steep path from the south. As Sardis's citizens sat atop their mountain post, they grew overconfident. After all, they figured, their city was impregnable.

Yet in 546 BC Sardis fell to Cyrus. Herodotus, the "father of history," records the defeat:

> Now the taking of Sardis came about as follows: When the fourteenth day came after Crœsus began to be besieged, Cyrus sent horsemen to announce to his army that he would give gifts to the first man to scale the wall. After this the army made an attempt. When it failed, they all ceased from the attack, except a certain Mardian named Hyroiades. He attempted to approach the side of the citadel where no guard had been set. [The Lydians] had no fear that it would ever be taken from that side, because there the citadel was precipitous and unassailable. . . . The previous day Hyroiades saw how one of the Lydians had descended on that side of the citadel to recover his helmet, which had rolled down, and that soldier descended to pick it up. Hyroiades took thought and cast the matter about in his own mind. Then he himself ascended. And after him came up others of the Persians, and many having thus made approach. So Sardis was finally taken and the whole city was given up to plunder.[21]

To the church in Sardis, Jesus warns, "I will come like a thief, and you will never know at what hour I will come against you" (Rev. 3:3). Sardis's citizens knew only too well about sudden, unexpected destruction. Their ancestors had thought they were safe when they were actually in great danger. Jesus rebukes the church at Sardis because, despite their reputation for being alive, they really were dead.

"An unguarded strength is actually a double weakness," wrote Oswald Chambers in *My Utmost for His Highest*.[22] Sometimes we shore up our weaknesses yet fail to reinforce our strengths. Then temptation knocks at the back door, and we shock ourselves when we fail.

---

[21] Herodotus, *Histories* 1.84.
[22] Oswald Chambers, *My Utmost for His Highest*, *"April 19."* 61st ed. Uhrichsville, Ohio: Barbour Books, 2010.

Think of your spiritual strengths. Have you grown complacent? What's your reputation? Maybe it was true once, but you now rest on an image created long ago. How old is your most recent testimony? Does the thought of Jesus' return bring joy or alarm? Wake up! Stay alert. Strengthen what remains.

MONDAY: REPUTATION VS. REALITY

1. Pray for the Spirit to grant you insight; then read Revelation 3:1–6:

> **3:1** To the angel of the church in Sardis write the following:
>
> "This is the solemn pronouncement of the one who holds the seven spirits of God and the seven stars: 'I know your deeds, that you have a reputation that you are alive, but in reality you are dead. **3:2** Wake up then, and strengthen what remains that was about to die, because I have not found your deeds complete in the sight of my God. **3:3** Therefore, remember what you received and heard, and obey it, and repent. If you do not wake up, I will come like a thief, and you will never know at what hour I will come against you. **3:4** But you have a few individuals in Sardis who have not stained their clothes, and they will walk with me dressed in white, because they are worthy. **3:5** The one who conquers will be dressed like them in white clothing, and I will never erase his name from the book of life, but will declare his name before my Father and before his angels. **3:6** The one who has an ear had better hear what the Spirit says to the churches.'"

2. In this message, what description of Jesus do you find?

_____

_____

What commendation for the church?

_____

_____

What criticism?

_____

_____

What consequence and exhortation?

_____

_____

What promise to the one who conquers?

_____

_____

Use your answers to fill in the chart at the beginning of this book. Also locate Sardis on the map.

3. How is Jesus described (3:1)?

_____

_____

• *The seven spirits of God* (3:1). As mentioned earlier, four times in Revelation we see reference to the seven spirits of God. This does not mean the Trinity has expanded to include Father, Son, and seven spirits! Some think the reference to seven spirits refers to characteristics of God (a spirit of discernment, a spirit of wisdom, etc.). They base their conclusion on this verse from Isaiah:

> **Isaiah 11:2** "The Lord's spirit will rest on him—
> a spirit that gives extraordinary wisdom,
> a spirit that provides the ability to execute plans,
> a spirit that produces absolute loyalty to the Lord."

Another possibility is that the spirits before the throne are Christ's angel-messengers (the Greek word can be translated either as *angel* or *messenger*) who receive the word from the Lord for each of the churches.

4. In one word or phrase, how would you summarize the church at Sardis? Give a reason for your answer.

_____

_____

5. Elsewhere, as in Isaiah 29:13, God described his spiritually dead people. List their characteristics.

> **Isa. 29:13** "The sovereign master says,
> 'These people say they are loyal to me;
> they say wonderful things about me,
> but they are not really loyal to me.
> Their worship consists of
> nothing but man-made ritual.'"

_____

_____

6. How are these characteristics evident in some churches today? (Bear in mind that the repetition many consider ritualistic might have originally been designed to communicate to an illiterate audience.)

_____

_____

7. Are any of these characteristics true of you? If so, in what way?

_____

_____

8. What do you learn about God and his character from this letter to Sardis? (For example, what does this passage tell you about what offends him? What does he desire for his people? What does the letter tell you about his desire to reward them and about his justice?)

_____

_____

9. If people could hear your thoughts, would they find your inner and outer life congruent, or would they see you projecting an external image of yourself that's more spiritual than you really are? Explain your answer.

_____

_____

10. In his first letter to the Corinthian church, Paul characterizes three types of people (1 Cor. 2:14–3:3). How do the three types of people differ?

> **2:14** "The unbeliever does not receive the things of the Spirit of God, for they are foolishness to him. And he cannot understand them, because they are spiritually discerned. **2:15** The one who is spiritual discerns all things, yet he himself is understood by no one. **2:16** *For who has known the mind of the Lord, so as to advise him?* But we have the mind of Christ.
>
> **3:1** So, brothers and sisters, I could not speak to you as spiritual people, but instead as people of the flesh, as infants in Christ. **3:2** I fed you milk, not solid food, for you were not yet ready. In fact, you are still not ready, **3:3** for you are still influenced by the flesh. For since there is still jealousy and dissension among you, are you not influenced by the flesh and behaving like unregenerate people?"

_____

_____

11. Which of these three types of people do you see in the church at Sardis? Explain your answer.

_____

_____

12. Which of the three types of people do you see in yourself?

_____

_____

13. Review your answers to questions 7, 9, and 12. For what do you need to pray for yourself based on your answers?

_____

_____

14. Spend time praying that the Lord will guard you from hypocrisy and fill your life with His Spirit. If it will help you focus, write out your prayer here.

_____

_____

Tuesday: Keeping Up Appearances

1. Begin your time in the Word with prayer; then read Revelation 3:1–2:

> **3:1** To the angel of the church in Sardis write the following: "This is the solemn pronouncement of the one who holds the seven spirits of God and the seven stars: 'I know your deeds, that you have a reputation that you are alive, but in reality you are dead. **3:2** Wake up then, and strengthen what remains that was about to die, because I have not found your deeds complete in the sight of my God.'"

2. What was Jesus' rebuke to the church at Sardis?

_____

_____

3. What do you think "You have a reputation that you are alive, but in reality you are dead" means?

_____

_____

4. Why does Jesus say, "I have not found your deeds complete"? Do you think this means the Christians in Sardis needed more works, or that something was missing from the works they did, or both? Consider the following passage:

> **1 Cor. 3:12** "If anyone builds on the foundation with gold, silver, precious stones, wood, hay, or straw, **3:13** each builder's work will be plainly seen, for the Day will make it clear, because it will be revealed by fire. And the fire will test what kind of work each has done. **3:14** If what someone has built survives, he will receive a reward. **3:15** If someone's work is burned up, he will suffer loss. **16** He himself will be saved, but only as through fire."

_____

_____

5. Compare the church at Sardis to the scribes and Pharisees described in Matthew 23:27–28. What similarities do you see?

> **23:27** "Woe to you, experts in the law and you Pharisees, hypocrites! You are like whitewashed tombs that look beautiful on the outside but inside are full of the bones of the dead and of everything unclean. **23:28** In the same way, on the outside you look righteous to people, but inside you are full of hypocrisy and lawlessness."

_____

_____

6. How does a church die, and what are some symptoms of decline?

_____

_____

7. Do decreasing numbers always indicate a dying church or ministry? Explain your answer.

_____

_____

8. What observations about spiritual aliveness can you make from the following passages?

> **John 6:63** "The Spirit is the one who gives life; human nature is of no help!"

....

> **John 7:37–39** "On the last day of the feast, the greatest day, Jesus stood up and shouted out, 'If anyone is thirsty, let him come to me, and **7:38** let the one who believes in me drink. Just as the scripture says, "*From within him will flow rivers of living water.*"' **7:39** (Now he said this about the Spirit, whom those who believed in him were going to receive, for the Spirit had not yet been given, because Jesus was not yet glorified.)"

....

> **John 15:5**—"I am the vine; you are the branches. The one who remains in me—and I in him—bears much fruit, because apart from me you can accomplish nothing."

_____

_____

9. Describe the Spirit-filled life according to Ephesians 5:15–21.

> **5:15** "Therefore be very careful how you live—not as unwise but as wise, **5:16** taking advantage of every opportunity, because the days are evil. **5:17** For this reason do not be foolish, but be wise by understanding what the Lord's will is. **5:18** And do not get drunk with wine, which is debauchery, but be filled by the Spirit, **5:19** speaking to one another in psalms, hymns, and spiritual songs, singing and making music in your hearts to the Lord, **5:20** always giving thanks to God the Father for each other in the name of our Lord Jesus Christ, **5:21** and submitting to one another out of reverence for Christ."

_____

_____

10. List things that tend to impress us when we look at churches and other believers.

_____

_____

11. How does your list line up with what God says he values?

_____

_____

12. When you sing in church, do you focus on how you sound or on Christ? Do you text or check phone messages or write your grocery list when you should have your attention focused on adoration or time in the Word? What steps can you take to keep your mind and heart fully focused on Christ?

_____

_____

13. In what ways can we keep from going through the motions in our spiritual practices?

_____

_____

14. For what would you say your own church is best known?

_____

_____

15. Do you think your church is in danger of becoming a dead church? Why or why not? (No names, please.)

_____

_____

16. Choose one servant in your church to encourage this week. What can you do to reinforce what is Spirit-led?

_____

17. When you serve others, do you do so out of your own abilities, or do you seek to work in partnership with the Holy Spirit?

_____

_____

18. Meditate on John 6:63: "The Spirit is the one who gives life; human nature is of no help!"

WEDNESDAY: WAKE UP AND WORK OUT

1. Pray for wisdom and insight in your time in the Word today; then read Revelation 3:1–3:

> **3:1** To the angel of the church in Sardis write the following: "This is the solemn pronouncement of the one who holds the seven spirits of God and the seven stars: 'I know your deeds, that you have a reputation that you are alive, but in reality you are dead. **3:2** Wake up then, and strengthen what remains that was about to die, because I have not found your deeds complete in the sight of my God. **3:3** Therefore, remember what you received and heard, and obey it, and repent. If you do not wake up, I will come like a thief, and you will never know at what hour I will come against you.'"

• *Wake up* (3:2). First Jesus describes the church in Sardis as dead (3:1). But then he tells them to wake up (v. 2). We see a similar link between sleep and death, between awakening and rising, in Ephesians 5:14:

> "Awake, O sleeper!
> Rise from the dead,
> and Christ will shine on you!"

Both the references in Ephesians and the one in Revelation are probably composite creations from Messianic verses in Isaiah:

> **Isa. 26:19** "Your dead will come back to life;
> your corpses will rise up.
> Wake up and shout joyfully, you who live in the ground!
> For you will grow like plants drenched with the morning dew,
> and the earth will bring forth its dead spirits."

Isa. 51:17 "Wake up! Wake up!
Get up, O Jerusalem!
You drank from the cup the Lord passed to you,
which was full of his anger!
You drained dry
the goblet full of intoxicating wine."

. . . .

Isa. 52:1 "Wake up! Wake up!
Clothe yourself with strength, O Zion!
Put on your beautiful clothes,
O Jerusalem, holy city!
For uncircumcised and unclean pagans
will no longer invade you."

. . . .

Isaiah 60:1 "Arise! Shine! For your light arrives!
The splendor of the Lord shines on you!"

2. List the five commands Jesus gives to the church in Sardis (Rev. 2:2–3).

_____

_____

3. Jesus exhorts the church at Sardis to "strengthen what remains" (3:2). Other translations say "strengthen the things that remain." What things would be vital to the life of a church to prevent it from dying?

_____

_____

_____

4. How would a church strengthen these things?

_____

_____

_____

5. Jesus says that he will "come like a thief" (3:3). Consider the typical response to a thief's arrival. In what way will Jesus' coming be like a thief to those "sleeping," according to this verse?

_____

_____

6. Usually the coming of Christ is presented as a joyous event for the believer. Yet according to the message to the church at Sardis, for some it could be a time of destruction. Are you prepared or unprepared for Jesus' return?

_____

_____

7. Compare Jesus' exhortation to the church at Ephesus (2:5) and the church at Sardis. What similarities do you see?

> **2:5** "Therefore, remember from what high state you have fallen and repent! Do the deeds you did at the first; if not, I will come to you and remove your lampstand from its place—that is, if you do not repent."
>
> . . . .
>
> **3:2** "Wake up then, and strengthen what remains that was about to die, because I have not found your deeds complete in the sight of my God. **3:3** Therefore, remember what you received and heard, and obey it, and repent. If you do not wake up, I will come like a thief, and you will never know at what hour I will come against you."

_____

_____

8. What differences do you see?

_____

_____

9. Imagine you were serving with the church at Sardis. How would you help them "wake up"?

_____

_____

10. Jesus exhorts the church at Sardis to remember what they have received and heard. Of the things you have seen and heard, what things do *you* need to remember?

_____

_____

11. How do we reach the place where we forget what we've seen and heard from God?

_____

_____

12. Near the end of his life, Moses addressed the children of Israel, challenging them to choose life over death. As you look at Moses' words from Deuteronomy 30:15–20, list all he commanded them to do:

> **30:15** "Look! I have set before you today life and prosperity on the one hand, and death and disaster on the other. **30:16** What I am commanding you today is to love the Lord your God, to walk in his ways, and to obey his commandments, his statutes, and his ordinances. Then you will live and become numerous and the Lord your God will bless you in the land which you are about to possess. **30:17** However, if you turn aside and do not obey, but are lured away to worship and serve other gods, **30:18** I declare to you this very day that you will certainly perish! You will not extend your time in the land you are crossing the Jordan to possess. **30:19** Today I invoke heaven and earth as a witness against you that I have set life and death, blessing and curse, before you. Therefore choose life so that you and your descendants may live! **30:20** I also call on you to love the Lord your God, to obey him and be loyal to him, for he gives you life and enables you to live continually in the land the Lord promised to give to your ancestors Abraham, Isaac, and Jacob."

_____

_____

13. According to verse 20, what is involved in choosing life?

_____

_____

14. Like a rolling inner tube, the spiritual life does not stand still. We're either going backward or forward. Are you pressing on, alive in Christ? Or are you sleeping? Are you talking with him? Participating in worship? Filled with his word? Applying what you've learned? Remembering what you've been taught? Participating in the life of his community? Reaching out with the good news? Denying yourself? Repenting in areas where you've fallen asleep?

_____

_____

15. Do you need to take steps to strengthen what remains? If so, what?

_____

_____

THURSDAY: CLEAN LAUNDRY

1. Pray for the Spirit to guide your time in his Word today; then read Revelation 3:4–5:

> **3:4** "But you have a few individuals in Sardis who have not stained their clothes, and they will walk with me dressed in white, because they are worthy. **3:5** The one who conquers will be dressed like them in white clothing, and I will never erase his name from the book of life, but will declare his name before my Father and before his angels."

2. For what does Jesus commend this church?

_____

_____

3. What do you think Jesus means when he describes the remnant in Sardis as those "who have not stained their clothes"?

_____

_____

• *Stained* (3:4). We find a form of this word two other times in the New Testament. In 1 Corinthians 8:7, we read about how one who offers meat sacrificed to idols can have a conscience that's *defiled*. In Revelation 14:4, we read about virgins who are not *defiled* with women.

4. Describe a time when you were a minority in a situation. How did it feel? What pressure did you experience?

_____

_____

5. In what ways are you tempted to have your "clothes" stained by the world around you?

_____

_____

6. How can someone remain strong in the faith when surrounded by unbelievers or by professing Christians who compromise?

_____

_____

7. To be holy means to be set apart. This does not always mean physical distance. It can simply mean we're different—in a good way—from everyone around us. What steps do you need to take in the Spirit to live a holy life?

8. Do you feel negative peer pressure more from unbelievers or from those who claim to follow Christ? Explain your answer.

9. How would the following promises encourage a remnant of faithful believers in a dead church?

> **Mal. 3:16–18** "Then those who respected the Lord spoke to one another, and the Lord took notice. A scroll was prepared before him in which were recorded the names of those who respected the Lord and honored his name. 'They will belong to me,' says the Lord who rules over all, 'in the day when I prepare my own special property. I will spare them as a man spares his son who serves him. Then once more you will see that I make a distinction between the righteous and the wicked, between the one who serves God and the one who does not.'"

> **1 Cor. 15:58** "So then, dear brothers and sisters, be firm. Do not be moved! Always be outstanding in the work of the Lord, knowing that your labor is not in vain in the Lord."

> **Heb. 6:10–12** "For God is not unjust so as to forget your work and the love you have demonstrated for his name, in having served and continuing to serve the saints. But we passionately want each of you to demonstrate the same eagerness for the fulfillment of your hope until the end, so that you may not be sluggish, but imitators of those who through faith and perseverance inherit the promises."

10. In what situations have you felt or do you feel spiritually isolated?

_____

_____

11. What specific steps can you take to find others who will help you live a life that's unstained by the world?

_____

_____

_____

_____

12. God said he will never leave us (Hebrews 13:5). That is how we can stand alone—because God is with us. The Lord spoke the following words to the nation of Israel thousands of years ago, but they are still true today:

> *"Others may, you cannot."* Many Christians find themselves reciting these words. Sometimes other believers can participate with clear consciences in activities that would make us feel guilty. The Spirit, not other people, dictates what we can and cannot do.

> **Isa. 41:10** "Don't be afraid, for I am with you!
> Don't be frightened, for I am your God!
> I strengthen you—
> yes, I help you—
> yes, I uphold you with my saving right hand!"

Thank God that he is with you every step of the way. Spend time in prayer, asking him to keep you clean in a dirty world.

FRIDAY: THE WARDROBE PROMISES

1. Pray for the Spirit to speak to you during your time in the Word today; then read Revelation 3:4–6:

> **3:4** "But you have a few individuals in Sardis who have not stained their clothes, and they will walk with me dressed in white, because they are worthy. **3:5** The one who conquers will be dressed

like them in white clothing, and I will never erase his name from the book of life, but will declare his name before my Father and before his angels. **3:6** The one who has an ear had better hear what the Spirit says to the churches."

2. What three things does Jesus promise to those who have not stained their clothes and to those who conquer?

_____

_____

_____

3. According to these passages, what is the significance of being clothed in white?

> **Rev. 3:18** "Take my advice and buy gold from me refined by fire so you can become rich! Buy from me white clothing so you can be clothed and your shameful nakedness will not be exposed, and buy eye salve to put on your eyes so you can see!"

....

> **Rev. 7:9** "After these things I looked, and here was an enormous crowd that no one could count, made up of persons from every nation, tribe, people, and language, standing before the throne and before the Lamb dressed in long white robes, and with palm branches in their hands. **7:10** They were shouting out in a loud voice, 'Salvation belongs to our God, to the one seated on the throne, and to the Lamb!' **7:11** And all the angels stood there in a circle around the throne and around the elders and the four living creatures, and they threw themselves down with their faces to the ground before the throne and worshiped God, **7:12** saying, 'Amen! Praise and glory, and wisdom and thanksgiving, and honor and power and strength be to our God for ever and ever. Amen!' **7:13** Then one of the elders asked me, 'These dressed in long white robes—who are they and where have they come from?' **7:14** So I said to him, 'My lord, you know the answer.' Then he said to me, 'These are the ones who have come out of the great tribulation. They have washed their robes and made them white in the blood of the Lamb! **7:15** For this reason they are before the throne of God, and they serve him day and night in his temple, and the one seated on the throne will shelter them. **7:16** *They will never go hungry or be thirsty again, and the sun will not beat down on them, nor any*

burning heat, **7:17** because the Lamb in the middle of the throne will shepherd them and lead them to springs of living water, *and God will wipe away every tear from their eyes.'"*

....

Rev. 19:7 "Let us rejoice and exult
and give him glory,
because the wedding celebration of the Lamb has come,
and his bride has made herself ready.

19:8 She was permitted to be dressed in bright, clean, fine linen" (for the fine linen is the righteous deeds of the saints)."

• *I will never erase his name from the book of life* (Rev. 3:5). Some have taken the promise of a perpetual name in the book of life to conversely imply Christ-followers can lose their salvation. Yet in fact Jesus seems to be promising the opposite. We find the word translated here as *erase* in four other instances in the New Testament (emphasis added):

"Therefore repent and turn back so that your sins may be **wiped out**" (Acts 3:19).

"He has **destroyed** what was against us, a certificate of indebtedness expressed in decrees opposed to us. He has taken it away by nailing it to the cross" (Col. 2:14).

"The Lamb in the middle of the throne will shepherd them and lead them to springs of living water, and God will **wipe away** every tear from their eyes" (Rev. 7:17).

"He will **wipe away** every tear from their eyes, and death will not exist any more—or mourning, or crying, or pain, for the former things have ceased to exist" (Rev. 21:4).

Notice that the first two instances relate to what happens at salvation. When someone repents and turns to Christ for salvation, all that person's sins are wiped out. Through Jesus' finished work, God destroys the list of judgments against that person. And the one who overcomes will never be removed from the list of those who are God's. So here's the question that often follows: What about the one who claims to follow Christ but does not overcome?

Often when we doubt our salvation (or that of others), we assure ourselves by thinking back and asking, *Was there a day when I accepted Jesus as my Savior?* If we answer yes, we breathe a sigh of relief, confident in the assurance of our salvation. Yet while we can never lose our salvation, the New Testament teaching would encourage us to ask a different question at such moments: *Has the Spirit changed me?*

We should each ask ourselves, Am I bearing fruit? Do I love others with my actions? Does my faith prompt me to act? If we can't answer positively, we should get nervous—not because we've lost our salvation, but because we need to *repent*. When we read Revelation's warnings, we're supposed to engage in self-examination. While God wants us to rest assured of his promise to save, he also wants us to tremble if we live like the world. Eight times in the Book of Revelation, we read that the one who has ears to hear had better listen to the words of this revelation (2:7, 11, 17, 29; 3:6, 13, 22; 13:9). That's some strong warning language. The message is not "Repent or lose your salvation." It's more like "Repent and *prove* your salvation."

4. Are you concerned about your standing with God? If you have never trusted in Christ alone for salvation, pray and tell him that you desire to do so right now. If you have already trusted Christ, ask the Spirit to search your heart and reveal any unconfessed sin. Repent and receive forgiveness. Then ask for the grace to be an overcomer, a conqueror.

5. Are you concerned about someone who has professed to trust Christ but whose lifestyle suggests otherwise? After confessing your own sins, pray fervently that he or she will repent. Then pray about whether the Spirit would have you lovingly confront that person. If you've already done so one-on-one, consider taking another witness with you.

6. What do you think it means when Jesus says of the one who conquers that he, Jesus, "will declare his name before my Father and before his angels" (Rev. 3:5)? Consider also Matthew 10:32.

> **10:32** "Whoever, then, acknowledges me before people, I will acknowledge before my Father in heaven."

7. How does Jesus' letter to the church at Sardis encourage and challenge you in your walk with God?

_____

_____

8. What observations concerning salvation and eternal security can you make from 1 Peter 1:3–9?

> **1:3** "Blessed be the God and Father of our Lord Jesus Christ! By his great mercy he gave us new birth into a living hope through the resurrection of Jesus Christ from the dead, **1:4** that is, into an inheritance imperishable, undefiled, and unfading. It is reserved in heaven for you, **1:5** who by God's power are protected through faith for a salvation ready to be revealed in the last time. **1:6** This brings you great joy, although you may have to suffer for a short time in various trials. **1:7** Such trials show the proven character of your faith, which is much more valuable than gold—gold that is tested by fire, even though it is passing away—and will bring praise and glory and honor when Jesus Christ is revealed. **1:8** You have not seen him, but you love him. You do not see him now but you believe in him, and so you rejoice with an indescribable and glorious joy, **1:9** because you are attaining the goal of your faith—the salvation of your souls."

_____

_____

9. What warnings about living the Christian life do you find in these verses?

> **James 1:22** "But be sure you live out the message and do not merely listen to it and so deceive yourselves. **1:23** For if someone merely listens to the message and does not live it out, he is like someone who gazes at his own face in a mirror. **1:24** For he gazes at himself and then goes out and immediately forgets what sort of person he was. **1:25** But the one who peers into the perfect law of liberty and fixes his attention there, and does not become a forgetful listener but one who lives it out—he will be blessed in what he does. **1:26** If someone thinks he is religious yet does not bridle his tongue, and so deceives his heart, his religion is futile. **1:27** Pure and undefiled religion before God the Father is this: to care

for orphans and widows in their misfortune and to keep oneself unstained by the world."

. . . .

2:14 "What good is it, my brothers and sisters, if someone claims to have faith but does not have works? Can this kind of faith save him? **2:15** If a brother or sister is poorly clothed and lacks daily food, **2:16** and one of you says to them, 'Go in peace, keep warm and eat well,' but you do not give them what the body needs, what good is it? **2:17** So also faith, if it does not have works, is dead being by itself. **2:18** But someone will say, 'You have faith and I have works.' Show me your faith without works and I will show you faith by my works. **2:19** You believe that God is one; well and good. Even the demons believe that—and tremble with fear."

10. Read aloud Revelation 7:9–17; then describe your ultimate future. Spend some time praising God as you meditate on these verses:

Rev. 7:9 "After these things I looked, and here was an enormous crowd that no one could count, made up of persons from every nation, tribe, people, and language, standing before the throne and before the Lamb dressed in long white robes, and with palm branches in their hands. **7:10** They were shouting out in a loud voice,

'Salvation belongs to our God,
to the one seated on the throne, and to the Lamb!'

7:11 And all the angels stood there in a circle around the throne and around the elders and the four living creatures, and they threw themselves down with their faces to the ground before the throne and worshiped God, **7:12** saying,

'Amen! Praise and glory,
and wisdom and thanksgiving,
and honor and power and strength
be to our God for ever and ever. Amen!'

7:13 Then one of the elders asked me, 'These dressed in long white robes—who are they and where have they come from?' **7:14** So I said to him, 'My lord, you know the answer.' Then he said to me, 'These are the ones who have come out of the great tribulation. They have washed their robes and made them white in the blood of the Lamb! **7:15** For this reason they are before the throne of God, and they serve him day and night in his temple, and the one seated on the throne will shelter them. **7:16** *They will never go hungry or be thirsty again, and the sun will not beat down on them, nor any burning heat,* **7:17** because the Lamb in the middle of the throne will shepherd them and lead them to springs of living water, and *God will wipe away every tear from their eyes.'"*

SATURDAY: CLOTHED IN WHITE

My older sister's husband, Gordon, was killed in 2009 by a hit-and-run driver who was texting. Riding in a bike lane, our beloved Gordy was making a ten-mile commute home from work on a sunny afternoon in Vancouver, Washington. Yet his helmet was not enough to save him when a driver mowed him down from behind and left him on the asphalt to die. Amazingly, of all the places to die along that long commute, Gordon passed into the Lord's presence on the street adjacent his own church.

My sister and my niece, whose carpool "meeting place" was their church's parking lot, were driving home when they came upon the traffic backup. They assumed they'd hit construction—until they inched closer. Then they recognized the mangled bike and the lone shoe in the middle of the road.

Mr. P. or simply P, as Gordon was called by his high school students, was known for standing outside his classroom door in his white lab coat between classes. As students rushed by, he'd call out to them, "I love ya—in a positive sort of way!" Today that phrase is painted in bold letters near the room where he taught thousands of science students.

The night after he died (on a Wednesday), about a hundred kids stood around in the rain at a makeshift memorial—until they received an invitation to join others inside the sanctuary who were remembering Gordon's life. On Wednesday nights Gordon had been known as his alter ego, Gordon the Science Warden, complete with white lab coat. He was supposed to teach that night, in fact. Instead, the group gathered to mourn—yet not as those without hope.

Through their tears that night, my niece and nephews stood on stage and shared the gospel. And afterward a student told my sister, "On my first day of high school, I planned to go home and kill myself. But Mr P. saw me in the hall, and since he didn't recognize me, he said, 'Hey! What's your name?'"

"Jennifer," the student responded.

"Hey, Jennifer," Gordon said. "I love ya—in a positive sort of way." Jennifer added with tears in her eyes: "Mr. P saved my life."

The day after Gordon died, something remarkable happened. I wrote an e-mail to thank a reporter for writing a well-written piece about Gordon's death, and he shot back with this: "Need to head over to high school as there are reports it's covered in white."

White blouses, white shirts, white sweat suits, white bandanas—whatever white apparel students had, they wore to honor P. And that Thursday night they organized an impromptu candlelight vigil in Mr. P's honor. Want to guess what color everybody wore?

And the funeral? It was held in the gym of the public school where Gordon kept a Bible on his desk, hoping students might ask about it. And as we sat in our white dresses, shirts, and lab coats, more than a thousand people heard about the source of Gordon's love—Jesus Christ.

Our clothing can make a statement. P's students wore white to say something about how much they esteemed their science teacher. But for Gordon's family members who love Christ and who know someday we will again see our brother in the faith, our white clothes reminded us of something far greater: "The one who conquers will be dressed like them in white clothing." Amen. Maranatha!

Pray: Almighty God, help us, your children, to overcome the world. Help us to stay on guard, prepared for the day when your Son returns. May that day be soon—may your kingdom come and your will be done on earth, as it is in heaven. Thank you that you are sovereign over all events—the grievous and the joyous. Thank you that you love those you ransomed with Jesus' blood. Grant us lives of purity and courage. Help us to tell others of your justice, mercy, power, strength, and love. As the hymn says, "Oh, for grace to trust [you] more . . ." In Jesus' name, Amen.

Memorize: "The one who conquers will be dressed like them in white clothing, and I will never erase his name from the book of life, but will declare his name before my Father and before his angels" (Rev. 3:5).

WEEK 7 OF 8

Philadelphia: The Little-Strength Church
Revelation 3:7–13

Scripture: "The one who conquers I will make a pillar in the temple of my God, and he will never depart from it" (Rev. 3:12).

Have you ever been in an earthquake? My younger sister has. When she lived in Northern California, she was standing in a car dealership when she felt vibrations and heard rattling. She thought someone was closing the huge metal doors through which cars enter and exit the showroom. But then she saw the closed doors and realized the *earth* was quaking.

In 2010 an earthquake devastated Chile. One witness wrote about experiencing it from the fifteenth floor of his apartment building. "The floor was moving around and around—[it was like] standing dead center in a swiftly spinning merry-go-round, trying to keep your balance. The television started moving, as did the bed, and I could hear glass shattering from other parts of my apartment. I couldn't quite stay on my feet, bouncing off the edge of my bed to my feet, then losing my

166

balance and falling again. I could hear furniture crashing, and from the kitchen cutlery clattered about like a pocketful of coins. I had a clear view out my picture window when all of a sudden, all the street lights snapped off all at once, while my building kept on whirling."[23]

Only weeks earlier, an earthquake in Haiti had rocked the Caribbean. An eyewitness described her experience. "Terrible rumbling, violent, shaking started, throwing me on the floor across the room. Right away the ceiling, walls, rocks, boards came crashing down, blocking the door. I thought my arm was broken. I focused, knowing I needed to get out. I dug myself out and climbed up on stuff. So many screaming. I did not make contact with [my husband] until that night. Sleeping is very difficult for everyone. Every noise, movement, we jump up. The aftershocks are scary. Last night I felt at least three with stuff rattling in our home. I don't think I slept at all. We are sleeping in the living room with the front door wide open."[24]

The citizens of ancient Philadelphia were well acquainted with such experiences. In AD 17 an enormous earthquake flattened their city, with multiple aftershocks that kept the people quaking after the tremors stopped. Such quakes were common events, resulting in a larger-than-usual percentage of people living outside the city walls. Better to risk danger from attackers, they reasoned, than to be crushed to death by falling debris.

Philadelphia, considered the gateway to Asia Minor, sat nestled against a hillside about thirty miles southeast of Sardis. The king of Pergamum founded it about 250 years before John wrote to the church there. The town received its name from the king's own nickname, *Philadelphus*, or "brother-lover, because the king was known for his special devotion to his brother, Eumenes II.

The city of Alasehir now sits on the site, and its earliest church remains date to the AD 600 Church of Saint John. All that's left of the structure are huge pillars. How significant, though, that John wrote to the tiny remnant in Philadelphia, "The one who conquers I will make a pillar in the temple of my God, and he will never depart from it" (3:12).

In an earthquake about the only thing left standing is the pillars. And Jesus promised Philadelphia's inhabitants that they could dwell

---

[23] Tyler Druden, "The Chilean Earthquake From A First Person Perspective," February 27, 2010, <www.zerohedge.com/article/guest-post-chilean-earthquake-first-person-perspective>, accessed March 5, 2010.

[24] Personal correspondence with the author.

inside the future heavenly temple and never again depart. Imagine how this promise sounded to the remnant of believers struggling in the face of adversity. The city is safe! You can stay inside the temple without facing danger of attack or debris. What security! What hope! Though their current life was filled with trials, God promised that a time was coming when they would never be shaken.

What's shaking you today? What threatens to split the foundations of your faith? Take heart. The Spirit wants to give you the strength to conquer. In fact, a day is coming when you will never have to run in fear. In your new home, his temple, you will live in safety forever.

MONDAY: THE ONE IN CHARGE SPEAKS

1. Pray for the Spirit's insight; then read Revelation 3:7–13:

> **3:7** To the angel of the church in Philadelphia write the following: "This is the solemn pronouncement of the Holy One, the True One, who holds the key of David, who opens doors no one can shut, and shuts doors no one can open: **3:8** 'I know your deeds. (Look! I have put in front of you an open door that no one can shut.) I know that you have little strength, but you have obeyed my word and have not denied my name. **3:9** Listen! I am going to make those people from the synagogue of Satan—who say they are Jews yet are not, but are lying—Look, I will make them come and bow down at your feet and acknowledge that I have loved you. **3:10** Because you have kept my admonition to endure steadfastly, I will also keep you from the hour of testing that is about to come on the whole world to test those who live on the earth. **3:11** I am coming soon. Hold on to what you have so that no one can take away your crown. **3:12** The one who conquers I will make a pillar in the temple of my God, and he will never depart from it. I will write on him the name of my God and the name of the city of my God (the new Jerusalem that comes down out of heaven from my God), and my new name as well. **3:13** The one who has an ear had better hear what the Spirit says to the churches.'"

2. In this message, what description of Jesus do you find?

_____

_____

What commendation for the church?

_____

_____

What criticism?

_____

_____

What consequence and exhortation?

_____

_____

What promise to the one who conquers?

_____

_____

Use your answers to fill in the chart at the beginning of this study. Also locate Philadelphia on the map.

3. As you read Jesus' message to Philadelphia, what stands out to you about this church? What is your overall impression?

_____

_____

4. In the previous five letters, the description of Jesus came from the vision recorded in Revelation 1:12–18. In this letter, however, the description comes from a different source, having distinct Old Testament features. How is Jesus described (3:7)?

_____

_____

• *The key of David* (3:7). This phrase comes from Isaiah 22:20–25, where the key to the house of David was given to Eliakim. To learn about Eliakim, we rewind back to the time of Israel's kings. After the kingdom split, Eliakim became governor under King Hezekiah (v. 20). We learn the functions of his office in an oracle of Isaiah in which Eliakim's predecessor is deposed and Eliakim takes his place (vv. 15–21). Eliakim is then made treasurer or steward "over the house." His royal clothing includes a robe and girdle, the insignia of his office. Once the government is committed to him, he is described as "father to the inhabitants of Jerusalem, and to the house of Judah" (v. 21, NASB). On his shoulder is laid the key of the house of David, giving him alone the power to open and shut—a symbol of his absolute authority to act as the king's representative (v. 22). We see the importance of his office from 2 Kings 15:5, where we read that King Azariah was smitten with leprosy, and Jotham, his heir, was over the household, judging the people of the land (2 Kings 15:5).[25]

Here's the Old Testament passage from which Jesus borrows his imagery when speaking to Philadelphia. The Lord is speaking to the unfaithful governor:

> **Isa. 22:20** "'At that time I will summon my servant Eliakim, son of Hilkiah. **22:21** I will put your robe on him, tie your belt around him, and transfer your authority to him. He will become a protector of the residents of Jerusalem and of the people of Judah. **22:22** I will place the key to the house of David on his shoulder. When he opens the door, no one can close it; when he closes the door, no one can open it. **22:23** I will fasten him like a peg into a solid place; he will bring honor and respect to his father's family. **22:24** His father's family will gain increasing prominence because of him, including the offspring and the offshoots. All the small containers, including the bowls and all the jars will hang from this peg. **22:25** At that time,' says the Lord who commands armies, 'the peg fastened into a solid place will come loose. It will be cut off and fall, and the load hanging on it will be cut off.' Indeed, the Lord has spoken."

In the Book of Hebrews, we see this same household imagery used to describe Jesus Christ:

> **3:5** "Now Moses was *faithful in all God's house* as a servant, to testify to the things that would be spoken. **3:6** But Christ is faithful as a son over God's house. We are of his house, if in fact we hold firmly to our confidence and the hope we take pride in."

---

[25] International Standard Bible Encyclopedia, Bible Works 4.0, CD-ROM, "Eliakim."

5. Based on the information just provided about "the key of David," what do you think Jesus is implying in Revelation when he says he "holds the key of David" and has the power to "open and shut"?

_____

_____

6. Why do you think it would encourage the church at Philadelphia that no one can shut a door Jesus has opened?

_____

_____

7. We have seen that one who governs holds keys and has authority. As possessor of the key of David, Jesus is the One whom the prophets foretold as having an eternal dynasty. So Jesus has authority over God's house. And Jesus knows what is happening to the church in Philadelphia. What does Jesus' authority paired with his knowledge of the faithfulness of his children suggest about their future?

_____

_____

8. Jesus is described also as "the Holy One, the True One" (3:7). How would you define the attributes of holiness and truth, and why do you think we find them paired here?

_____

_____

9. Which of Jesus' attributes referenced in Revelation 3:7 most encourages you today and why?

_____

_____

10. How did Isaiah respond to God's holiness in Isaiah 6:1–8?

6:1 "In the year of King Uzziah's death, I saw the sovereign master seated on a high, elevated throne. The hem of his robe filled the temple. **6:2** Seraphs stood over him; each one had six wings. With two wings they covered their faces, with two they covered their feet, and they used the remaining two to fly. **6:3** They called out to one another, 'Holy, holy, holy is the Lord who commands armies! His majestic splendor fills the entire earth!' **6:4** The sound of their voices shook the door frames, and the temple was filled with smoke. **6:5** I said, 'Too bad for me! I am destroyed, for my lips are contaminated by sin, and I live among people whose lips are contaminated by sin. My eyes have seen the king, the Lord who commands armies.' **6:6** But then one of the seraphs flew toward me. In his hand was a hot coal he had taken from the altar with tongs. **6:7** He touched my mouth with it and said, 'Look, this coal has touched your lips. Your evil is removed; your sin is forgiven.' **6:8** I heard the voice of the sovereign master say, 'Whom will I send? Who will go on our behalf?' I answered, 'Here I am, send me!'"

_____

_____

11. How do you view God's character? Do you ever doubt that he has authority, is just, holy, or true? If so, why?

_____

_____

12. Take account of your own character. Are you just? holy? true? In what areas do you struggle with these attributes?

_____

_____

13. Why do you think Jesus provides such a description of himself before going on to tell the church in Philadelphia what he knows about them?

_____

_____

14. Spend a few moments thinking about the character of Christ. Give thanks for his authority, justice, holiness, and truth. Pray for yourself that he will conform you to his image.

TUESDAY: NEVER, EVER, EVER GIVE IN!

1. Pray that the Spirit will grant you insight and a tender heart today; then read Revelation 3:8–10.

> **3:8** "I know your deeds. (Look! I have put in front of you an open door that no one can shut.) I know that you have little strength, but you have obeyed my word and have not denied my name. **3:9** Listen! I am going to make those people from the synagogue of Satan—who say they are Jews yet are not, but are lying—Look, I will make them come and bow down at your feet and acknowledge that I have loved you. **3:10** Because you have kept my admonition to endure steadfastly, I will also keep you from the hour of testing that is about to come on the whole world to test those who live on the earth."

2. What two things does Jesus say he knows about this church?

_____

_____

3. How would this knowledge encourage them?

_____

_____

4. What does Jesus say the enemies of the Philadelphia church will ultimately acknowledge, and what will be their body language as they do so (3:9)?

_____

_____

5. Why would this promise encourage the church?

_____

_____

6. For what three things does Jesus commend the Philadelphian church?

_____

_____

7. What connection do you see between their deeds and Jesus' authority (3:8)?

_____

_____

8. Why would having "little strength" be a positive and not a negative?

_____

_____

9. What were the circumstances in which the Philadelphian church had to persevere?

_____

_____

10. What similarities do you see in the church at Philadelphia and the church at Smyrna (2:8–11)?

> **2:8** To the angel of the church in Smyrna write the following: "This is the solemn pronouncement of the one who is the first and the last, the one who was dead, but came to life: **2:9** 'I know the distress you are suffering and your poverty (but you are rich). I also know the slander against you by those who call themselves Jews and really are not, but are a synagogue of Satan. **2:10** Do not be afraid of

the things you are about to suffer. The devil is about to have some of you thrown into prison so you may be tested, and you will experience suffering for ten days. Remain faithful even to the point of death, and I will give you the crown that is life itself. **2:11** The one who has an ear had better hear what the Spirit says to the churches. The one who conquers will in no way be harmed by the second death.'"

11. How is the promise to Philadelphia about the synagogue of Satan even better than the one to Smyrna?

_____

_____

12. Jesus commends the church at Philadelphia for its obedience. Is it possible to obey without loving him? Is it possible to love without obeying him? (See also John 14:23–24.) Explain your answer.

> **John 14:23** "Jesus replied, 'If anyone loves me, he will obey my word, and my Father will love him, and we will come to him and take up residence with him. **14:24** The person who does not love me does not obey my words. And the word you hear is not mine, but the Father's who sent me.'"

_____

_____

13. What are some circumstances in your life in which you need to persevere?

_____

_____

14. How does Jesus' message to the church in Philadelphia encourage you to press on?

_____

_____

15. Spend some time being honest with God about your trying or overwhelming circumstances. Perhaps the suffering is not your own, but you care for another who is in deep pain. Entrust the situations to Jesus Christ. Ask him to grant you perseverance, working in and through you to accomplish his purpose.

WEDNESDAY: THE ETERNAL WEIGHT OF GLORY

1. Pray that the Spirit will grant you insight into his Word; then read Revelation 3:8–10:

> **3:8** "I know your deeds. (Look! I have put in front of you an open door that no one can shut.) I know that you have little strength, but you have obeyed my word and have not denied my name. **3:9** Listen! I am going to make those people from the synagogue of Satan—who say they are Jews yet are not, but are lying—Look, I will make them come and bow down at your feet and acknowledge that I have loved you. **3:10** Because you have kept my admonition to endure steadfastly, I will also keep you from the hour of testing that is about to come on the whole world to test those who live on the earth."

2. What had Jesus done for this church (v. 8)?

_____

_____

3. According to John 10:9 and Acts 14:27, what is one possible meaning of the phrase, "I have put before you an open door which no one can shut"?

> **John 10:9** "I am the door; if anyone enters through Me, he shall be saved, and shall go in and out, and find pasture."
>
> ....
>
> **Acts 14:27** "When they arrived and gathered the church together, they reported all the things God had done with them, and that he had opened a door of faith for the Gentiles."

_____

_____

4. What would be another possible meaning according to the following verses?

> **1 Cor. 16:8–9** "But I will stay in Ephesus until Pentecost, because a door of great opportunity stands wide open for me, but there are many opponents."

....

> **2 Cor. 2:12** "Now when I arrived in Troas to proclaim the gospel of Christ, even though the Lord had opened a door of opportunity for me . . ."

....

> **Col. 4:3** "At the same time pray for us too, that God may open a door for the message so that we may proclaim the mystery of Christ, for which I am in chains."

_____

_____

• *I have loved you* (Rev. 3:9). In Malachi 1:2 we read that God made an argument against Israel. They had questioned his love because their enemies were defeating them, and as a result they showed God disrespect and doubted. So he reminded them of the many ways in which he had been faithful to them. God's people often try to find a clear cause-and-effect relationship between sin and suffering. And in Revelation, we find such a situation. In Philadelphia some Jews probably thought themselves superior, thinking the Christ-followers were suffering because of their faith in Jesus. And to this suffering remnant the Lord promised to humble their accusers and vindicate the weak.

5. Because of their faithfulness and obedience, what did Jesus promise this church (3:10)?

_____

_____

6. Notice the scope of that hour of testing. What is its purpose, and who will be affected?

_____

_____

7. In light of your answer to the previous question, why might the "hour of testing" or "hour of trial" (NIV) refer to the seven-year period of trial commonly known as the Great Tribulation rather than an isolated, temporary period of testing?

_____

_____

8. If the "open door that no one can shut" refers to the Judge rescuing the church from future judgment, what does it suggest about their eternal security?

_____

_____

9. How might the truth that they are eternally secure help them persevere?

_____

_____

10. What do you learn about God's character from Jesus' promises here?

_____

_____

11. Do you ever lose sight of the end? Being faithful to the Savior is worth any difficulty we might face now because the end far outweighs the present challenges. Meditate on 2 Corinthians 4:17–18: "For our momentary, light suffering is producing for us an eternal weight of glory far beyond all comparison because we are not looking at what can be seen but at what cannot be seen. For what can be seen is temporary, but what cannot be seen is eternal."

_____

_____

12. What "momentary, light suffering" are you currently facing?

_____

_____

13. What does God say is true of your future?

_____

_____

14. Spend some time thanking God for his provision for your future in Jesus Christ.

THURSDAY: HE'S COMING SOON

1. Pray for the Spirit to reveal the Jesus, the Truth, to you; then read Revelation 3:11–13:

> **3:11** "I am coming soon. Hold on to what you have so that no one can take away your crown. **3:12** The one who conquers I will make a pillar in the temple of my God, and he will never depart from it. I will write on him the name of my God and the name of the city of my God (the new Jerusalem that comes down out of heaven from my God), and my new name as well. **3:13** The one who has an ear had better hear what the Spirit says to the churches."

2. Today we will focus on Revelation 3:11. Jesus tells the Philadelphian church that he is coming soon. How does Jesus' coming here differ from the comings he refers to in the previous letters to we have looked at?

> **Rev. 2:5** "Therefore, remember from what high state you have fallen and repent! Do the deeds you did at the first; if not, I will come to you and remove your lampstand from its place—that is, if you do not repent."
> . . . .
> **Rev. 2:16** "Therefore, repent! If not, I will come against you quickly and make war against those people with the sword of my mouth."
> . . . .

Rev. 3:3 "Therefore, remember what you received and heard, and obey it, and repent. If you do not wake up, I will come like a thief, and you will never know at what hour I will come against you."

· ·

Rev. 3:11 "I am coming soon. Hold on to what you have so that no one can take away your crown."

_____

_____

3. What insight does this different coming give us about the church in Philadelphia?

_____

_____

4. Jesus exhorts the Philadelphian church to "Hold on to what you have so that no one can take away your crown." He is not referring to salvation but to rewards. In light of the parable in Luke 19:11–27, what is one possible meaning and cause of someone "[taking] away your crown"?

19:11 "While the people were listening to these things, Jesus proceeded to tell a parable, because he was near to Jerusalem, and because they thought that the kingdom of God was going to appear immediately. **19:12** Therefore he said, 'A nobleman went to a distant country to receive for himself a kingdom and then return. **19:13** And he summoned ten of his slaves, gave them ten minas, and said to them, "Do business with these until I come back." **19:14** But his citizens hated him and sent a delegation after him, saying, "We do not want this man to be king over us!" **19:15** When he returned after receiving the kingdom, he summoned these slaves to whom he had given the money. He wanted to know how much they had earned by trading. **19:16** So the first one came before him and said, "Sir, your mina has made ten minas more." **19:17** And the king said to him, "Well done, good slave! Because you have been faithful in a very small matter, you will have authority over ten cities." **19:18** Then the second one came and said, "Sir, your mina has made five minas." **19:19** So the king said to him, "And you are to be over five cities." **19:20** Then another slave came and said, "Sir, here is your mina that I put away for safekeeping in a piece of cloth. **19:21** For I was afraid of you, because you are a severe man. You withdraw what you did not deposit and reap what you did not sow." **19:22** The king said to him, "I will judge you by your own words, you wicked slave! So you knew, did you, that I was a severe man, withdrawing what I didn't deposit and reaping what I didn't sow? **19:23** Why then didn't you put my money in the bank, so that when I returned I could have collected it with interest?" **19:24** And he said to his attendants, "Take the mina from him, and give it to the one who has ten." **19:25** But they said to him, "Sir, he has ten minas already!" **19:26** I tell you that everyone who has will be given more, but from the one who does not have, even what he has will be taken away. **19:27** But as for these enemies of mine who did not want me to be their king, bring them here and slaughter them in front of me!'"

---

5. Losing the crown could also refer to rewards lost because we embrace worldly values that keep us from growing in our faith. What are some negative influences that could cause you to lose your crown?

---

6. What steps are you taking or can you take, by the aid of the Holy Spirit, to reduce the influence of worldly values in your life?

---

7. Jesus instructed the churches at Thyatira and Philadelphia to "hold on." What makes it difficult for you to hold on?

---

8. Writing to the Thessalonian Christians, Paul speaks of a time when Jesus will return (1 Thess. 5:6–11). What instructions does he give for how believers are to live until then?

> **5:6** "So then we must not sleep as the rest, but must stay alert and sober. **5:7** For those who sleep, sleep at night and those who get drunk are drunk at night. **5:8** But since we are of the day, we must stay sober by *putting on the breastplate* of faith and love and as *a helmet* our hope *for salvation*. **5:9** For God did not destine us for wrath but for gaining salvation through our Lord Jesus Christ. **5:10** He died for us so that whether we are alert or asleep we will come to life together with him. **5:11** Therefore encourage one another and build up each other, just as you are in fact doing."

_____

_____

9. If you knew Jesus would return today, what would you do?

_____

_____

10. Would you stand with confidence or shrink away at his coming? Why?

_____

_____

11. What, if anything, needs to change in your priorities and choices so the thought of Jesus' return is the sweetest thought imaginable?

_____

_____

12. How can the thought of Jesus' return bring hope to your current circumstances?

_____

_____

13. Talk to God about your priorities. Ask him to help you and your fellow Christians hold fast. Tell him about your friends who need him too.

1. Pray for the Spirit's guidance; then read Revelation 3:12–13:

> **3:12** "The one who conquers I will make a pillar in the temple of my God, and he will never depart from it. I will write on him the name of my God and the name of the city of my God (the new Jerusalem that comes down out of heaven from my God), and my new name as well. **3:13** The one who has an ear had better hear what the Spirit says to the churches."

2. What does Jesus promise to the one who conquers (3:12)?

_____

_____

- *A pillar in the temple* (3:12). Pillars from King Solomon's temple in Jerusalem have been found to bear inscriptions of their architects' or donors' names (see also 1 Kings 7:21). In the New Testament, Paul says that at the time he and Barnabas set out to reach the Gentiles, Peter, James, and John seemed to be the "pillars" among Jewish Christians. Later Paul speaks of the church—the household of God—as the pillar and support of truth (1 Tim. 3:15, NASB). For someone to be called a pillar had positive associations, as it does now. Probably because of this biblical imagery, we sometimes say, "He is a pillar in the community" or "She is a pillar in the church."

But the idea in Revelation probably goes beyond honor. Strabo, the Greek geographer who lived from 63 BC to AD 24, wrote this: "In Philadelphia . . . not even the walls are safe, but in a sense are shaken and caused to crack every day. And the inhabitants are continually attentive to the disturbances in the earth and plan all structures with a view to their occurrence".[26] Temple pillars in this part of the world were built to withstand earthquakes, so they stood for decades,

[26] Strabo, *Geography*, 12.18.

if not centuries. The Philadelphian Christians probably saw the pillars in their city as the only remaining structures—the only things that endured in a time of great trial. With this in mind, consider that Jesus promises he will build an eternal city with the ones who overcome in Philadelphia as its pillars.

3. Have you ever experienced an earthquake or known someone who has? If so, what was it like?

_____

_____

• *He will never depart from it* (3:12). The Greek here uses two negations, in the same way we might say "Not! No way. "It has a strong emphatic force—"not *even* gonna happen." At the end of the phrase is also a word we can translate "yet" or "again," so many translations render this, "He [who overcomes or conquers] will never depart again." Now, imagine a world without building codes. In an earthquake, where would people want to run when the foundations trembled? Outside! Where would they want to sleep? In tents rather than in houses that could bury them in bricks and logs. The wise person goes *out* and stays out. Yet here Jesus promises that the conqueror in the temple of God will never, ever depart. To people who had taken to the open country to escape the unsafe city, the promise that they would never again have to leave their city would come as a wonderful picture of hope, stability, and security.

4. In your own words, how might the symbolism of pillars and never departing be especially meaningful to the Philadelphian Christians?

_____

_____

5. Reread the promise to Sardis about their names enduring (3:5) along with the description of Philadelphia's overcomers as inscribed pillars (3:12). What similarities and contrasts do you see?

> **3:5** "The one who conquers . . . I will never erase his name from the book of life, but will declare his name before my Father and before his angels."

3:12 "The one who conquers I will make a pillar in the temple of my God, and he will never depart from it. I will write on him the name of my God and the name of the city of my God (the new Jerusalem that comes down out of heaven from my God), and my new name as well."

_____

_____

6. What three names does Jesus promise to write on the pillars, the ones who overcome (3:12)?

_____

_____

7. What do you think having the three names "engraved" implies?

_____

_____

8. To Christ-followers in a city rocked by destruction, insecurity and fear, God promises a future of rebuilding, stability, and peace. What instabilities and fears are you facing today?

_____

_____

9. Spend a few moments surrendering your fears to God. Ask him to grant you the peace that passes understanding.

10. What worship songs or psalms can you load onto your CD or MP3 player to focus your mind on Jesus, the Truth? If you are doing this study as part of a group, consider asking your group for recommendations.

_____

_____

11. Life is unstable. Yet a secure dwelling place exists for the one who conquers. When we read of the future for the persevering believer, we find many metaphors and symbols. We know little about the eternal state in terms of what it will literally be like. We simply know it's wonderful beyond anything we can imagine. Which of the images that you've studied so far brings you the most hope and comfort as you seek to overcome and conquer?

_____

_____

12. Each letter to the churches ends with this warning: "The one who has an ear had better hear what the Spirit says to the churches" (3:13). Notice that that last word in this quote is plural. What does this suggest about the intended audience for all the letters?

_____

_____

13. Jesus Christ gives his message to each church in Revelation, yet we read after each message that the one speaking to the churches is the Spirit. What does this suggest about the unity of Christ and the Spirit?

_____

_____

_____

SATURDAY: SMALL BUT MIGHTY

When seminary student Ben Stuart graduated from college, he had visions of doing ministry on a large scale. When a start-up church hired him as the only staff member in addition to the pastor, he found himself employed as a youth pastor of one student. Only one! This experience, he says, "was a severe blow to my ego—thanks be to God—and it pushed me toward a deeper dependence on Jesus."

Today Ben serves thousands of college students at a major Texas university. Every week they fill a coliseum to hear his Bible teaching. Yet he retains his sincere passion for the lone individual.

We all know such a passion for the individual reflects the heart of God if we believe Jesus' story about the lost sheep and the shepherd who would leave the ninety-nine to seek the one. And remember when God appeared to Elijah? He did so not in the wind, earthquake, or fire but in the sound of gentle blowing, a still, small voice (1 Kings 19:12).

We can't always measure the Spirit's work by the numbers, can we?

Sad to say, my husband and I had our own experience learning to value the "small." One summer long ago we taught a Sunday school class for college students. One week only four students showed up, so we canceled the class. Afterward our kind and godly pastor took us aside and admonished us to decrease our vision. Our actions, he said, suggested we were measuring success by numbers, assuming the turn-out was an accurate measure of God's blessing—or lack thereof. If four people came to us hungry to learn about the Lord, he told us, we had a great chance to provide individual instruction. What an opportunity we had squandered!

In John's Gospel we read that a large group of followers ultimately left Jesus. He asked his disciples, "Will you also go away?" (John 6:67, NKJV). Surely we don't assume from Jesus' dwindling numbers that he lacked the Spirit's approval, do we?

Particularly in America, we tend to measure a church by the size of its sanctuary or its radio ministry or its television outreach. Members seeking to impress others sometimes mention the name of their semi-famous pastor more than they "drop" the name of Jesus. The church at Philadelphia stands as a reminder to us to stop such foolishness: Jesus says to them, "I know that you have little strength, but you have obeyed my word and have not denied my name" (Rev. 3:8). They were small but mighty. And that's often the case—that the Spirit is in the small. Of all the churches in the Book of Revelation, the one with little strength received Jesus' highest praise.

Are you gauging success—yours and others'—by external factors? Do you feel depressed that God seems to bless others' efforts but not your own? Or perhaps you have the opposite struggle. Maybe you're smugly thinking you have the Spirit's approval because you're enjoying great numbers or great accolades.

Humble yourself under the mighty hand of God. Ask him to make you strong in him. Pray for the insight to see beyond externals to the unseen domain of what truly lasts. Humans look at the outside; God looks at the heart.

Pray: Lord Jesus, please touch my eyes as you did those of the blind man. Open them to gaze not on what I can see with human eyes, but on the eternal realities seen only by having your perspective. Help me to remember your blessings to come and to live in light of them. Thank you for your promise of comfort and security to all who endure. You are my rock, my foundation, my pillar, my ceiling, my temple, my house, my home. To you be the glory forever. Amen.

Memorize: "I am coming soon. Hold on to what you have so that no one can take away your crown" (Rev. 3:11).

WEEK 8 OF 8

Laodicea: The Lukewarm Church
Revelation 3:14–22

If someone asked me to name five materially wealthy people, I'd probably answer, "Oprah, Bill Gates, Warren Buffett, Mary Kate and Ashley Olsen." Maybe I'd replace the twins with Madonna and Johnny Depp, but my point is that I could come up with a list fairly quickly. Yet what if I were asked to name 150 rich people? I couldn't do it. I certainly wouldn't think of naming myself, my husband, my daughter, my parents, my sister, my nieces and nephews, my cousins, my pastor . . .

Am I materially wealthy? Is my church rich? Not if we compare ourselves with Donald Trump types. But what if we compare ourselves to my friends in the tribal village I visited last summer? Oh. Now, that's a different story. Hand me a church directory, and I'll just read you the first 150 names—including those on unemployment.

We might not feel like we're rich, but we are. We have clean water spewing through more than one faucet in every home while some of our African friends drink goats' blood mixed with milk so they can stay hydrated. It's a great alternative to filthy water, or no water at all.

We also know where our next meals are coming from. And if we get hungry, we have any number of family members, church members, and government agencies that will help us. By the grace of God, we have a huge safety net.

On the way home from Africa, my family talked about how even homeless people in our country can find potable water for free at libraries. Or at Walmart or city parks.

When my daughter gave her extra hard-boiled egg and half a sandwich to some of the village kids, they ran barefooted for two miles down the dirt road behind our car as we departed. They weren't begging. They were just waving good-bye to such a kind girl.

So materially we are more wealthy than we know, but spiritually we're more impoverished than we realize too. Jesus said, "Blessed are the poor in spirit" (Matt. 5:3). And the opposite of being poor in spirit is being self-sufficient. Ouch.

We think we can live the Christian life on our own. We think we're exercising our spiritual gifts, but we're actually just operating out of our natural strengths. Or our prayer lives show how little we depend on the Spirit. Or both. If we had eyes to see, we'd realize that, spiritually speaking, we're poorer than the orphans combing garbage dumps in search of not-too-rotten morsels.

The church at Laodicea had a little problem with self-sufficiency too. Their city was a strategic banking center known for its wealth. When an earthquake devastated it in AD 60, they rejected offers of aid from Rome and used their own wealth to pay for reconstruction. Now, that's rich! (Imagine New Orleans turning down government aid after Hurricane Katrina because they didn't need it.) And apparently the city's mentality influenced Laodicea's believers.

So Jesus told them, "You say, 'I am rich and have acquired great wealth, and need nothing,' but do not realize that you are wretched, pitiful, poor, blind, and naked" (Rev. 3:17). His solution? "Buy gold from me refined by fire so you can become rich" (v. 18).

Jesus wanted his followers to become rich. How can we do that? How can we who are poor buy what Jesus offers?

Spiritual wealth comes from dependency. We receive Jesus' riches by grace. We become rich by grace, and we stay rich by grace.

How many truly rich people do you know? Are you on the list? By grace you can be.

1. Pray for insight; then read the letter to the church at Laodicea (Rev. 3:14–22):

> **3:14** To the angel of the church in Laodicea write the following: "This is the solemn pronouncement of the Amen, the faithful and true witness, the originator of God's creation: **3:15** 'I know your deeds, that you are neither cold nor hot. I wish you were either cold or hot! **3:16** So because you are lukewarm, and neither hot nor cold, I am going to vomit you out of my mouth! **3:17** Because you say, "I am rich and have acquired great wealth, and need nothing," but do not realize that you are wretched, pitiful, poor, blind, and naked, **3:18** take my advice and buy gold from me refined by fire so you can become rich! Buy from me white clothing so you can be clothed and your shameful nakedness will not be exposed, and buy eye salve to put on your eyes so you can see! **3:19** All those I love, I rebuke and discipline. So be earnest and repent! **3:20** Listen! I am standing at the door and knocking! If anyone hears my voice and opens the door I will come into his home and share a meal with him, and he with me. **3:21** I will grant the one who conquers permission to sit with me on my throne, just as I too conquered and sat down with my Father on his throne. **3:22** The one who has an ear had better hear what the Spirit says to the churches.'"

2. In this message, what description of Jesus do you find?

_____

_____

What commendation for the church (if any)?

_____

What criticism?

_____

_____

What consequence and exhortation?

_____

_____

What promise to the one who conquers?

_____

_____

Use your answers to fill in the chart at the beginning of this book. Also, locate the Laodicea in ancient Asia Minor on the map.

3. How does the letter to Laodicea differ from the previous six letters? What is not included in this letter that is found in the other six?

_____

_____

4. This is not the first time the church at Laodicea appears in the Bible. Colossae was near Laodicea and even supplied it with water. What else do we learn about the church at Laodicea from the following verses?

Col. 2:1 "For I want you to know how great a struggle I have for you, and for those in Laodicea, and for those who have not met me face to face."

. . . .

Col. 4:12 "Epaphras, who is one of you and a slave of Christ, greets you. He is always struggling in prayer on your behalf, so that you may stand mature and fully assured in all the will of God. **4:13** For I can testify that he has worked hard for you and for those in Laodicea and Hierapolis. **4:14** Our dear friend Luke the physician and Demas greet you. **4:15** Give my greetings to the brothers and sisters who are in Laodicea and to Nympha and the church that meets in her house. **4:16** And after you have read this letter, have it read to the church of Laodicea. In turn, read the letter from Laodicea as well. **4:17** And tell Archippus, 'See to it that you complete the ministry you received in the Lord.'"

• *Pronouncement of the Amen* (3:14). The word *amen* means "truly" or "so be it" or "of a certainty." Here it appears as a description of the one speaking, Jesus himself, the true witness.

5. In addition to gaining an overview of Jesus' message, today we focus on the description of Jesus Christ himself. Here he is "the Amen, the faithful and true witness, the originator of God's creation" (3:14). How do the following verses give clarity to these titles?

Looking for more resources about the seven churches? Check out *Seven Deadly Spirits* by T. Scott Daniels. The author sees each church in Revelation as representing a key area of struggle for both the congregations addressed and also believers throughout church history. Ephesus is the spirit of boundary keeping; Smyrna, the spirit of consumerism; Pergamum, the spirit of coercive power; Thyatira, the spirit of privatized faith; Sardis, the spirit of prosperous ease; Philadelphia, the spirit of fear; and Laodicea, the spirit of self-sufficiency.

Isa. 65:16 "Whoever pronounces a blessing in the earth will do so in the name of the faithful God; whoever makes an oath in the earth will do so in the name of the faithful God. For past problems will be forgotten; I will no longer think about them."

. . . .

John 14:6 "Jesus replied, 'I am the way, and the truth, and the life. No one comes to the Father except through me.'"

. . . .

2 Cor. 1:20 "For every one of God's promises are 'Yes' in him; therefore also through him the 'Amen' is spoken, to the glory we give to God."

. . . .

Rev. 19:11 "Then I saw heaven opened and here came a white horse! The one riding it was called 'Faithful' and 'True,' and with justice he judges and goes to war."

• *The originator of God's creation* (3:14). The NASB translates this same phrase as "the beginning of God's creation." Others say "the ruler of God's creation." The Greek word they're all translating as "originator," "beginning," and "ruler" can have any of these meanings. But *beginning* has more of the sense of *origin* or *originator*. Think of how Jesus is also called the "Alpha and Omega, the Beginning and the End." That does not mean the second person of the Trinity had a beginning, as if God the Father created God the Son—that's heresy! We learn at the beginning of the Gospel of John that the Word was in the beginning with God and the Word was God, and the Word became flesh and dwelt among us (see John 1:1, 14). The *NET Bible* notes state that the standard Greek lexicon (dictionary) gives the meaning "the first cause" for the word in Rev 3:14, a term that is too philosophical for the general reader, so the translation "originator" was used instead.

6. Recall a time when you failed to keep a commitment, a confidence, a promise, or a vow. How do you think the offended person felt?

_____

_____

7. Jesus Christ has never failed to keep a commitment, backed out of a promise, or broken a vow, nor will he. What are some of the promises you're depending on him to keep? What would be some of the consequences for you if he were unfaithful?

_____

_____

8. Recall a time when you lied and got caught. How did that feel to you and to the person you lied to?

_____

_____

9. Jesus Christ has never lied. Ever. What would be some of the consequences for you if he were untrue?

_____

10. Worship him for being before all things, the Originator, the Amen, the Truth, the Faithful One.

1. Pray that the Lord will search your heart and reveal to you areas where you need to conform to his word; then read Revelation 3:15–17:

> **Rev. 3:15** "I know your deeds, that you are neither cold nor hot. I wish you were either cold or hot! **3:16** So because you are lukewarm, and neither hot nor cold, I am going to vomit you out of my mouth! **3:17** Because you say, 'I am rich and have acquired great wealth, and need nothing,' but do not realize that you are wretched, pitiful, poor, blind, and naked."

2. Describe the church in Laodicea.

_____

_____

3. What insight does verse 17 give us concerning the state of the church?

_____

_____

4. On the basis of what knowledge does Jesus pronounce his assessment that the church is lukewarm (v. 15)?

_____

_____

5. Why do you think Jesus Christ wishes what he does (v. 15)?

_____

_____

6. What is Jesus' response to lukewarm water (v. 16)? Why do you think he uses such strong imagery?

_____

_____

7. How would you recognize the state of being lukewarm in your church?

_____

_____

8. How would you recognize the state of being lukewarm in yourself?

_____

_____

9. Are you hot, cold, or lukewarm in your spiritual walk? Explain your answer.

_____

_____

10. What evidence do you find that the Laodicean church was guilty of self-sufficiency?

_____

_____

11. In what areas of your life do you lean toward self-sufficiency instead of looking to Christ's sufficiency?

_____

_____

12. Why do you think Jesus Christ describes the church in Laodicea as "wretched, pitiful, poor, blind, and naked"?

_____

_____

13. Jesus Christ alone is our sufficiency. Apart from him we can do nothing (John 15:5). Take some time today to reflect on your life and ask God to show you areas in which you are depending on yourself, others, or things for your sufficiency instead of him.

WEDNESDAY: GOING SHOPPING

1. Pray for insight; then read Revelation 3:18–19:

> **3:18** "Take my advice and buy gold from me refined by fire so you can become rich! Buy from me white clothing so you can be clothed and your shameful nakedness will not be exposed, and buy eye salve to put on your eyes so you can see! **3:19** All those I love, I rebuke and discipline. So be earnest and repent!"

2. What three things does Jesus advise the Laodiceans to put on their shopping list?

_____

_____

3. The city of Laodicea had a reputation for its wealth. Her citizens dressed in the fine black wool for which their city was known, and they also produced excellent eye salve. Yet Jesus suggests they are oblivious to their own need. In fact they think they're strong where he considers them deficient. How does Jesus say his gold, white clothing, and eye salve will help them?

_____

_____

4. From what you know of metals, how is gold refined by fire superior to unrefined gold?

_____

_____

5. Instead of the black garments popular in Laodicea, Jesus wanted the Laodiceans to purchase apparel from him—white clothing. You'll recall he promised that those in Sardis who overcome also will be dressed in white. How might the following passages shed additional light on Jesus' meaning?

> **Isa. 61:10** "I will greatly rejoice in the Lord; I will be happy because of my God. For he clothes me in garments of deliverance; he puts on me a robe symbolizing vindication. I look like a bridegroom when he wears a turban as a priest would; I look like a bride when she puts on her jewelry."
>
> ·
>
> **Rev. 7:9–11** "After these things I looked, and here was an enormous crowd that no one could count, made up of persons from every nation, tribe, people, and language, standing before the throne and before the Lamb dressed in long white robes, and with palm branches in their hands. **7:10** They were shouting out in a loud voice, 'Salvation belongs to our God, to the one seated on the throne, and to the Lamb!' **7:11** And all the angels stood there in a circle around the throne and around the elders and the four living creatures, and they threw themselves down with their faces to the ground before the throne and worshiped God."
>
> ·
>
> **Rev. 19:7–8** "Let us rejoice and exult and give him glory, because the wedding celebration of the Lamb has come, and his bride has made herself ready.
>
> **19:8** She was permitted to be dressed in bright, clean, fine linen (for the fine linen is the righteous deeds of the saints)."

_____

_____

_____

6. What link do you see between Revelation 3:18 and Revelation 19:8?

_____

_____

7. Based on Revelation 3:19, do you think Jesus is talking to believers or unbelievers?

_____

8. How can someone "buy" gold refined by fire, white garments, and eye salve in the way Christ means? What hint does verse 19 give you?

_____

_____

9. How might Isaiah 55:1–3 shed light on how to go on such a "shopping trip"?

> **55:1** "Hey, all who are thirsty, come to the water! You who have no money, come! Buy and eat! Come! Buy wine and milk without money and without cost!
>
> **55:2** Why pay money for something that will not nourish you? Why spend your hard-earned money on something that will not satisfy? Listen carefully to me and eat what is nourishing! Enjoy fine food!
>
> **55:3** Pay attention and come to me! Listen, so you can live!"

_____

_____

10. This passage reminds us that Jesus, not worldly things having no eternal value, is the source of true life and fulfillment. Jesus Christ warns all who are in danger of putting trust in the wrong things. In what areas of your life are you most tempted to do that?

_____

_____

11. Paul prayed for the church at Laodicea years before John wrote Jesus' message to them. What are Paul's prayer priorities for them according to Colossians 2:1–3?

> **2:1** "For I want you to know how great a struggle I have for you, and for those in Laodicea, and for those who have not met me face to face. **2:2** My goal is that their hearts, having been knit together in love, may be encouraged, and that they may have all the riches that assurance brings in their understanding of the knowledge of the mystery of God, namely, Christ, **2:3** in whom are hidden all the treasures of wisdom and knowledge."

_____

_____

12. Knowing what you now know about Laodicea's wealth, how might that affect your understanding of Paul's prayer?

_____

_____

13. Time to go shopping. Take stock of your life; then ask the Lord to give you true wealth, to grant you spiritual sight, and to clothe you with righteous deeds.

THURSDAY: TIME FOR DINNER

1. Pray for the Spirit to work in your life; then read Revelation 3:19–20.

> **3:19** "All those I love, I rebuke and discipline. So be earnest and repent! **3:20** Listen! I am standing at the door and knocking! If anyone hears my voice and opens the door I will come into his home and share a meal with him, and he with me. **3:21** I will grant the one who conquers permission to sit with me on my throne, just as I too conquered and sat down with my Father on his throne. **3:22** The one who has an ear had better hear what the Spirit says to the churches."

2. Why do you think Jesus interjects, "All those I love, I rebuke and discipline" at this point in the letter? That is, how does this assurance relate what Jesus has just said with what he is about to say?

_____

_____

3. How do rebuke and discipline play a role in loving someone?

_____

_____

4. If Jesus loves the church so much, why does he rebuke her?

_____

5. In Revelation 3:19, Jesus tells the Laodiceans to "be earnest and repent." Why is it necessary for them to be "zealous" (NASB) or "earnest" along with repentance?

_____

_____

6. In the Book of Ezekiel, the Lord speaks to the nation of Israel with this message:

> Ezek. 18:30 "Therefore I will judge each person according to his conduct, O house of Israel, declares the sovereign Lord. Repent and turn from all your wickedness; then it will not be an obstacle leading to iniquity. 18:31 Throw away all your sins you have committed and fashion yourselves a new heart and a new spirit! Why should you die, O house of Israel? 18:32 For I take no delight in the death of anyone, declares the sovereign Lord. Repent and live!"

What instructions does God give Israel concerning their sin and why?

_____

_____

7. How is Ezekiel's message similar to the one addressed to Laodicea? What do you learn about God?

_____

_____

8. Often we hear Revelation 3:20 quoted as a gospel invitation for unbelievers to come to Christ. In the original context of the letter to Laodicea, do you think this invitation was intended for unbelievers or believers? Explain your answer.

Repentance means we realize that in the presence of a holy God we fall short—far short. We're guilty as sin. And our attempts at our own self-help righteousness sicken God. We deserve His anger for our rebellion. We realize we're filled with sin, and we long to get rid of it—and not just partially, but in every possible shape and form. We renounce the world no matter what the cost, realizing Jesus is worth dying for and living for. We also renounce the world's mind and outlook as well as its practice. Then we deny our flesh, take up the cross, and follow hard after Christ.

_____

_____

_____

_____

_____

9. Was this invitation directed to individuals or to the church community? Or to both? Explain your answer.

_____

_____

• *I will come into his home and share a meal with him, and he with me* (3:20). Often people read this verse as a promise that Jesus will physically enter our bodies; hence the popular expression "Ask Jesus into your heart." I heard of a child who even felt his heartbeat and said, "I can feel him jumping up and down in there!" The Spirit, not the Son, indwells believers. The expression "come into" in the Greek does not mean entrance into a *person*. It means to enter a room or building and move toward a person. Many interpreters understand

Jesus to be inviting an entire church to intimate fellowship—a collective rather than individual invitation. That is not to say Jesus does not invite people to personal communion with him. It just means that is not necessarily what *this* verse teaches.

10. Elsewhere in his ministry, Jesus called himself the door of the sheep through which anyone who enters shall be saved (John 10:9). In that context Jesus *is* the door. Do you think it's appropriate to use a metaphor of Jesus standing *at* the door when talking with unbelievers about their spiritual need? If an exact metaphor does not appear in the Bible, can we still use it to illustrate? Explain your answer.

_____

_____

11. What steps can you take, led by the Spirit, to help your local group of believers move toward greater intimacy with Jesus Christ?

_____

_____

Friday: Graduating Summa Cum Laude

1. Pray for the Spirit to make his meaning clear to you; then read Revelation 3:20–22.

> **3:20** "Listen! I am standing at the door and knocking! If anyone hears my voice and opens the door I will come into his home and share a meal with him, and he with me. **3:21** I will grant the one who conquers permission to sit with me on my throne, just as I too conquered and sat down with my Father on his throne."

2. What does Jesus say he will grant to the one who conquers? (If this promise doesn't blow us away, something's wrong!)

_____

_____

3. What do the following verses add to our understanding that those who conquer will sit with Jesus on his throne?

> **Romans 8:16–17** "The Spirit himself bears witness to our spirit that we are God's children. And if children, then heirs (namely heirs of God and also fellow heirs with Christ—if indeed we suffer with Him so we may also be glorified with him."

....

> **Revelation 20:4–6** "Then I saw thrones and seated on them were those who had been given authority to judge. I also saw the souls of those who had been beheaded because of the testimony about Jesus and because of the word of God. These had not worshiped the beast or his image and had refused to receive his mark on their forehead or hand. They came to life and reigned with Christ for a thousand years. **20:5** (The rest of the dead did not come to life until the thousand years were finished.) This is the first resurrection. **20:6** Blessed and holy is the one who takes part in the first resurrection. The second death has no power over them, but they will be priests of God and of Christ, and they will reign with him for a thousand years."

_____

_____

4. What insight do these verses from the Book of Hebrews give concerning Jesus overcoming and being seated with the Father on his throne?

> **1:1** "After God spoke long ago in various portions and in various ways to our ancestors through the prophets, **1:2** in these last days he has spoken to us in a son, whom he appointed heir of all things, and through whom he created the world. **1:3** The Son is the radiance of his glory and the representation of his essence, and he sustains all things by his powerful word, and so when he had accomplished cleansing for sins, *he sat down at the right hand of the Majesty on high.* **1:4** Thus he became so far better than the angels as he has inherited a name superior to theirs."

....

> **8:1** "Now the main point of what we are saying is this: We have such a high priest, one who *sat down at the right hand of the throne of the Majesty in heaven.*"

....

12:2 "Keeping our eyes fixed on Jesus, the pioneer and perfecter of our faith. For the joy set out for him he endured the cross, disregarding its shame, and *has taken his seat at the right hand of the throne of God.*"

_____

_____

5. According to Revelation 3:21, is Jesus' "seated at the right hand of the throne of God" (Heb. 12:2) on an adjacent throne or is Jesus sharing the same throne?

_____

_____

6. Imagine what it will be like to share the kind of honor Jesus describes! What do you think that will be like?

_____

_____

7. Though Jesus' promises of reward won't happen until a future day, how can the honor he describes lend perspective to our current circumstances?

_____

_____

8. What lessons can we learn from the church at Laodicea that can help us overcome the world?

_____

_____

_____

9. Look back through your answers and think over what you've learned as you've studied Jesus' words to the seven churches. Each of the messages ends with the admonition to "hear what the Spirit says to the churches." What, if anything, is hindering you from responding to him based on what you've learned?

_____

_____

10. Have you made commitments during your study that still require action? If so, what?

_____

_____

11. Look back to pages 3–8 where all seven letters to the churches appear. Circle all references to works and deeds. Notice how important it is for Christ-followers to show our faith by our works.

_____

_____

12. How would you evaluate the effectiveness of the church in the world today and why?

_____

_____

13. What about your own church? How do you think Jesus would assess its health and why? (No names, please.)

_____

_____

_____

14. Do you see trends in churches that concern you? that cause you to rejoice?

_____

_____

15. Pray for yourself, your church, the churches in your community, and the body of Christ worldwide.

Scripture: "So because you are lukewarm, and neither hot nor cold, I am going to vomit you out of my mouth!" (Rev. 3:16).

If you live near Dallas, it's H-E-B—Hurst, Euless, Bedford. If you live near Seattle, it's Seattle, Bedford, Tacoma. Near the border of Tennessee and Virginia, it's Kingsport, Johnson City, and Bristol. Lots of states have their own tri-cities areas. And if you lived in first-century Asia Minor, a familiar tri-cities area would have been Colossae, Hierapolis, and Laodicea.

Laodicea, though wealthy, needed its neighbors' help, because it lacked one major resource—water. You wouldn't have known it just by looking around town, however, because everywhere in Laodicea people saw Roman baths, aqueducts, and fountains. But despite the cosmetic fix of multiple water-related structures, Laodicea required others' help for 100 percent of its water supply. That meant piping water several miles through underground aqueducts: Colossae sent cold mountain-stream water, and Hierapolis the runoff from its hot springs.

Now, think about that. Do you ever run water for a hot bath and have to wait for the pipes to warm before you can get the temperature you want? What about in the heat of summer? Do you ever turn on your faucet only to find the water too warm to refresh you? In Laodicea, because it had to travel so far through aqueducts, the water from Colossae and Hierapolis arrived brackish, foul, and tepid—lukewarm. Nobody ever got to guzzle cold water on a hot day in Laodicea. Ever.

I spent one blistering July day there—a day on which I accidentally left my water bottle on the bus. After a hike up the steps in the best-preserved ancient theater I've ever seen, followed by a trek up to the site where history says Philip was martyred, I panted for some liquid refreshment. So when I got back to the bus, I grabbed my water bottle and took a big swig.

Ble-e-e-e-ech!

Was that ever a mistake! After sitting in that hot bus all afternoon, my water was lukewarm. Gross! I wanted to spew it out.

In that moment I realized something of what Jesus meant when he told the Christians in Laodicea that their lukewarm temperature made him want to vomit.

I love cold lemonade on an August day. And I love a steaming mocha in the dead of winter. But tepid water makes me want to hurl year round. Jesus too, apparently.

I've heard it said the letter to Laodicea teaches us that it's better to be a "cold" Christian with no interest in spiritual things than to be a "lukewarm" Christian. But nothing could be farther from the truth. In his metaphor, Jesus uses both *cold* and *hot* as positives. Both temperatures in their places are pleasant and refreshing—but lukewarm is just plain awful.

Are you flaky or committed? Refreshing or repulsive? Sitting on the fence or standing up for your faith? What evidence do those around you see of your love for Jesus Christ? Does your Perrier make Jesus want to puke, or are you like a long drink of spring water that quenches his thirst?

Pray: Lord Jesus, thank you for redeeming me! I long for the day when I will see you face-to-face and we'll be free from the power of sin. I long for the day when I will see you sitting on the throne and I will bow at your feet in worship. I can hardly fathom the thought of your calling me up to enjoy that honor with you. Help me to overcome! Thank you that you discipline those you love, that you give opportunities to repent, that you're merciful and give me a second (and third and fourth . . .) chance. Thank you for the great future hope you offer your children. As I struggle on this earth in my fleshly body, help me press on to obedience out of love. Keep me from losing my first love, from being lukewarm, from being poor despite my wealth. Grant me the grace to trust you more and to show love for you by deeds done for your glory.

Memorize: "I will grant the one who conquers permission to sit with me on my throne, just as I too conquered and sat down with my Father on his throne" (Rev. 3:21).